SECOND LIFE

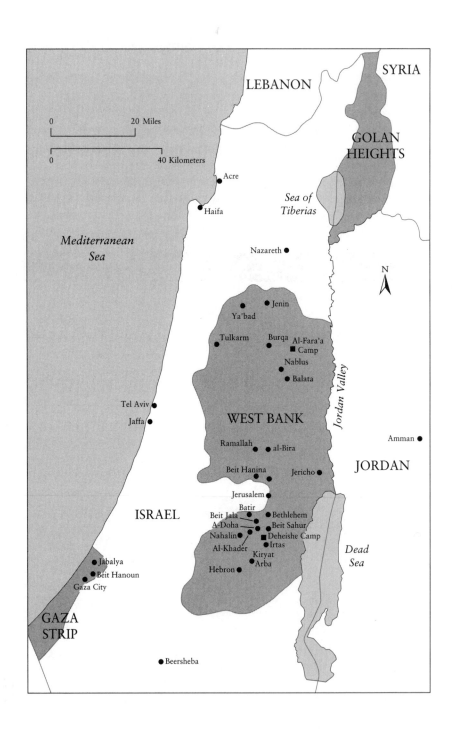

SYRIA

LEBANON

GOLAN
HEIGHTS

0   20 Miles

0   40 Kilometers

Acre

Sea of
Tiberias

Haifa

Mediterranean
Sea

Nazareth

N

Jenin

Ya'bad

Tulkarm   Burqa   Al-Fara'a
                         Camp
                    Nablus

                    Balata

Tel Aviv
Jaffa

WEST BANK   Jordan Valley

Ramallah   al-Bira   Amman

Beit Hanina   JORDAN
                Jericho

Jerusalem

ISRAEL   Batir
         Beit Jala   Bethlehem
         A-Doha   Beit Sahur
         Nahalin   Deheishe Camp
                 Irtas   Dead
         Al-Khader   Kiryat   Sea
                 Arba
Jabalya   Hebron
Beit Hanoun
Gaza City

GAZA
STRIP

Beersheba

Janet Varner Gunn

SECOND LIFE

A

West Bank

Memoir

Foreword by

Lila Abu-Lughod

University of Minnesota Press

Minneapolis & London

Excerpts from the following sources are reprinted with permission:
B'Tselem (the Israeli Information Center for Human Rights in the
Occupied Territories), material from the April 1990 Information Sheet;
Mary Curtius, "Wounded Palestinian Youth in Boston for Hospital Stay,"
Boston Globe, October 5, 1988; Mahmoud Darwish, "The Earth Is
Closing in around Us," in Victims of a Map, trans. Abdullah al-Udhari,
copyright 1984 Al Saqi Books; Avigdor Feldman, "Marwan Learns to Live
with a Marble in His Head," Hadashot, January 20, 1989, trans. courtesy
the Palestine Human Rights Information Center; James Graff,
memorandum of September 1988 to the International Committee of the
Red Cross regarding Mohammad Abu Aker; Law in the Service of Man
(Al-Haq), "Torture and Intimidation in the West Bank: The Case of Al
Fara'a Prison (Ramallah: Al Haq, 1985); Ori Nir, "The Uprising and the
Making of a Hero," Ha'aretz, October 7, 1988; the Palestine Human
Rights Information Center, Update, May 1, 1989; Michael Sela, "Kite
War," Jerusalem Post, July 10, 1989.

Published by the University of Minnesota Press
111 Third Avenue South, Suite 290, Minneapolis, MN 55401-2520
Printed in the United States of America on acid-free paper

Library of Congress Cataloging-in-Publication Data

Gunn, Janet Varner.

Second Life : a West Bank memoir / Janet Varner Gunn.
    p.   cm.
Includes bibliographical references (p.   ) and index.
ISBN 0-8166-2530-1
    1. West Bank—Politics and government. 2. Palestinian Arabs—
Civil rights—West Bank. 3. Duhayshah (Refugee camp) 4. Gunn,
Janet Varner—Journeys—West Bank. I. Title.
DS110.W47G86   1995
956.95'3044'092—dc20   95-13541

The University of Minnesota is an
equal-opportunity educator and employer.

For two sons:
Adam Gunn and Mohammad Abu Aker

Contents

The Abu Aker family

Malka (Um Nidal, the mother of Nidal)

Naim (Abu Nidal, the father of Nidal)

Nidal and Rafat, twin brothers, the eldest children

Mohammad, the "living martyr"

Hazem, the youngest brother

Nida', the family's first daughter

Hala, the second daughter and youngest child

"Our Blood Will Plant Its Olive Tree"
Lila Abu-Lughod

As the Palestinians find their way in a confusing new phase of their history of dispossession, Janet Varner Gunn's memoir of two years of the Intifada will stand as an eloquent and troubling record of a previous moment. She tells the story of this history in the making as she and the families in a particular place—the politically active Palestinian refugee camp near Bethlehem called Deheishe—lived it. The decision to tell her story in this form, as a memoir of daily life that interweaves her own memories with the experiences of people she came to know through her human rights work, makes this a book that speaks to more than the Palestinian situation. *Second Life* speaks both to the more general experience of what it means to be a "survivor" and to contemporary debates across the humanities and social sciences about forms of knowledge, modes of inquiry, and ways of writing.

In the Everyday

Much has been written on the Intifada, the uprising that began in late 1987 among the West Bank and Gaza Palestinians who had been living under Israeli military occupation for twenty years. Even more has been written on the question of Palestine and what goes by the name of "the Arab-Israeli conflict," of which the Intifada was but a small part. The books and articles devoted to this topic fill rows of library stacks, stuff research centers, and occupy busy scholars and partisans. Perspectives vary; opposing arguments seek to persuade. Yet these writings, for the most part, share one thing: they distance readers from the everyday lives of ordinary people making this history.

Gunn instead has chosen to privilege the everyday, the personal, the ordinary (although in the Palestinian case ordinary life takes some extraordinary forms). She wants to get behind what she calls the Big News: the deaths, injuries, punishments, land confiscations, and house demolitions that might be the currency of journalism or the documentation of human rights violations. But she also seems to want to get behind what we might call the Big Topics of scholarly political analysis: 1936, 1948, 1967, 1973, 1987, the British Mandate and the United Nations, blooming deserts, settler colonialism, expulsion, terrorism, the peace process, and so on.

We need to know the Big News; work on the Big Topics is invaluable. But neither can provide what is crucial in a conflict in which one side's suffering was for so long excluded from world concern and in which representations of a community have been so willfully distorted. Gunn intends *Second Life* to provide a much needed "discourse of familiarity" on the Palestinians. This discourse, I have argued in the somewhat different context of a critique of anthropological modes of writing, is an essential element in a humanism that is still our most powerful moral discourse against domination.[1]

Concerned about the politics of representation, I had explored in my book on women in a Bedouin community in Egypt how conventional ways of writing about people in other "cultures" might reinforce a sense of separation between "us" in the West and "them" elsewhere that would help underwrite larger structures of global inequality. I worried particularly about writing that worked through generalizing or typifying. Noting that we all live in the world of dailiness, even though the content of our days may be quite different, I suggested that a strategy of writing by focusing on individuals and the particulars of their lives might begin to undermine the pernicious reification of cultural difference.

Although I recognized that social scientific and other generalizing modes were just as often used in describing our own society in the United States as in writing about other societies, I argued that the distancing effect the writing produced was always balanced by the effects of other sorts of accounts. These were the familiar accounts in the ordinary language we use in personal conversations to discuss our lives, our friends and family, and our world. But these alternative and offsetting accounts hardly existed in the West for other communities, and so I thought perhaps we would do well to create them.

This is what *Second Life* has done. Gunn has constructed her narrative in the language of everyday events like a conversation with an old man in a room overlooking his garden, a sudden encounter with a mouse and an Israeli patrol while she was breaking curfew to feed some rabbits, and a young man's joking relationship with a piece of lifesaving medical machinery. She has constructed it around the teenager Mohammad Abu Aker, whom she met in 1988 as a serious bullet injury "case" and helped to obtain medical treatment in Boston, to whom she dedicates her book as a second son, whose two years as a "living martyr" of the Intifada she chronicles. She prevents us from forgetting, through this technique, that we are privileged to know something of the lives of people living elsewhere.

Ironically, by trying to get at the everyday and the ordinary, Gunn makes us see that ordinary people in different places are forced to live their lives in vastly different ways. The discourse of familiarity, of individuals and incidents of everyday life, actually enables us to grasp the specificity of the human. For the Palestinians of Deheishe in the late 1980s, this humanity involves living with the real possibilities of violent death—so much so that even when outside observers are pronouncing the Intifada over, Gunn reports that two of her friends remark, as she leaves for the United States and says she will see them in a year, that maybe they will be dead. It involves watching young boys who throw little stones being shot at the funerals of other youngsters. This humanity also involves hospital wards with fourteen-year-old boys whose lives are on the line, one paraplegic because a bullet passed through his spinal cord, one who has lost his finger while making the victory sign.

On a more mundane level, the specificity of the human means the ordinary disturbances and intrusions of house searches and identity card checks and the furtive visits home of young men on the run because they are on "the Bingo list," Israel's inventory of suspected activists. This had all become so much of the everyday that Gunn comments, "The enormity of the outrage under which Deheishe lived its ordinary life hit me full force only when I left Palestine for the familiar territory of home."

If suffering is a taken-for-granted part of everyday life for ordinary people, it is not paralyzing. Gunn notes that the Palestinians she knows do not make of suffering a badge of their humanity, as do the Jewish characters in Bernard Malamud's stories of the mundane. Instead, they seem to celebrate it in order to continue to fortify their resolve to continue resisting—often, as she says, by trying "to keep hold on the ordinary, no matter what." She tells of a woman who continued to cross-stitch the sleeve of her dress while her house was being raided and one who rolled grape leaves to feed the family under an extended curfew; she tells of people who marry and have children, who tend gardens and build houses. Most poignantly, she tells of children who fly kites even when Israeli soldiers shoot the kites down, of children who provoke soldiers to shoot round lead bullets coated in rubber so they can replenish supplies for marble games.

To be human and active, for the people Gunn knows in Deheishe, is also to be political. Death is that most human and universal of losses, but even that, in the camp, is made to take on a different meaning. Following the practice instituted during the Intifada, funerals of "martyrs" in Deheishe took on a novel form. There was crying and mourning, especially among the old women for whom this is unbreakable practice. But sweets were also distributed, as at a wedding. Most of the funeral activities involved family, neighbors, and friends, but delegations of political groups also came to pay their respects, and much of the energy of young mourners was spent making and arranging political banners, posters, plaques, and wooden shields. The bravest spray-painted graffiti—for which they could be shot on sight—under cover of darkness. Besides playing on loudspeakers the expected Koranic recitation, mourners sang or played patriotic political songs. Meanwhile, Israeli soldiers watched closely, entering houses at random moments to confiscate "mourning decorations" or shouting to request songs to which they could disco.

This chronicle of Deheishe shows that political activity was an everyday matter. Everyone seemed to be affiliated with a political faction and had a strategy or opinion about what should happen. In a telling scene, Gunn describes how Nasser, a young man of the camp, responded to a request from his older brother, now living in New Jersey, to write him letters about day-to-day life in the camp—leaving out the politics. "How," he asks, "can I keep politics out of my letters?"

Not all of this political activity is inspiring. Although the book has lessons to teach about the meaning of resistance and revolution, and the resilience of humanity in circumstances of persistent violence and political repression, Gunn does not shy away from some of the ugly effects of the

Situation, as Deheishe residents call it, on relations within the embattled community. She describes factional infighting and bickering. More pointedly, she writes openly about the problem of collaborators, not only revealing the tactics prisoners in Ansar III, the tent prison Israel set up in the Negev, used to expose them but also describing the shunning and even violence that is used to punish them in the camp. What is most troubling about this situation, as in many situations, is that women are dealt with more severely than men are.

What Gunn wants us to remember, though, is that she found a group of people who struggle and suffer but can still laugh and embrace others. Her stories of ordinary people clinging to life and refusing to give up or to leave—stories of what the Palestinians refer to as *sumud*, or steadfastness—remind me of the searing lines of a poem by Mahmoud Darwish.[2] This is the same poem from which the title of Edward Said's essay-memoir, *After the Last Sky*, was taken. That book, accompanied by Jean Mohr's striking photographs, speaks, like *Second Life*, of the everyday realities of Palestinian lives.[3] The poem opens with this line: "The earth is closing in around us, pushing us through the last passage and we tear off our limbs to pass through."

Gunn describes the limbs that people had to tear off: mothers who cut off tears so they will not despair after losing sons, fathers who cut off anger as they wait for the return of sons from prisons, neighbors who cut off friends when they are found to be collaborating with the Israeli authorities.

But Gunn also shows the young people of Deheishe echoing the image of the last line of Darwish's poem as they commemorate the martyrs of the Intifada with portraits that depict them with roots coming down into the earth. The life to which this suffering gives birth will last because it is rooted in the land. In Darwish's words, "We will die here, here in the last passage. Here or here our blood will plant its olive tree."

Situated Writing

In recent years feminist scholars, anthropologists, historians of science, and others have mounted a damning critique of the possibility of objectivity. Tracing the origins of all knowledge in particular perspectives, historical contingency, and partiality, they have gone further than earlier critics of objectivity in the social sciences by arguing that claims to objectivity are themselves political. Noting that only the powerful can pretend—and believe—that their own position is one of objectivity, that they hold the perspectiveless perspective, feminist scholars have been particularly good at questioning such claims. What Donna Haraway argues, however, is that we are able to make sustainable claims about the knowledge we produce *only* if we *care* about the world; we dare not fall into the relativism of care-*less* objectivity. Making a case for what she calls "situated knowledges," she calls for

> politics and epistemologies of location, positioning, and situating, where partiality and not universality is the condition of being heard to make rational knowledge claims. These are claims on people's lives; the view from a body, always a complex, contradictory, structuring and structured body, versus the view from above, from nowhere, from simplicity.[4]

Second Life is a wonderful illustration of the usefulness of situated knowledge. We never forget in this book how a view is always from somewhere and that what one sees—and is enabled to see and describe —depends on that somewhere. Gunn situates herself as an American, a woman, an academic, a human rights worker, and a long-ago little girl from Western Pennsylvania searching for something. She also situates herself squarely within the Palestinian camp of Deheishe, not outside it looking in over the twenty-foot fence meant to pen residents inside.

She self-consciously invokes situatedness by opening chapter 2 with a contrast between her own first impressions of Deheishe camp and those of David Grossman, the author of *The Yellow Wind*. Where he, a stranger and an Israeli Jew, saw in the rain ugly cement growths, empty grocery shelves, open sewers, and children with runny noses, she, an American human rights volunteer who had just paid one of many hospital visits to a young man from the camp, saw sunshine and a courtyard full of roses, geraniums, daisies, morning glories, and a glassed-in veranda offering panoramic views of Israeli soldiers patrolling the camp around the clock. Grossman described the refugee camp as a place of waiting and nostalgia. Gunn came to see Deheishe from inside the fence that surrounded the camp as a place of constant activity and ongoing lives.

She also positions herself differently from Jean Genet, whose autobiographical memoir of two years in the 1970s in a training camp for Palestinian fighters was posthumously published as *Prisoner of Love*. For the French writer, Gunn notes, the healing epiphany was a moment—did it ever happen?—when he stayed in a young man's room; the young man was away fighting, and his mother brought Genet coffee and a glass of water as she would have to her son. It was a moment of recovering the maternal love Genet, abandoned by his prostitute mother, had never had. Gunn too found healing in Palestine, but it was by stepping beyond the exoticism of Old Jerusalem's Jaffa Gate into the ordinary (but extraordinary) world of Deheishe.

Gunn comes to know some of the women in the camp, but she is never confined to their world. She moves back and forth between the men and the women, actually spending more of her time and learning more from conversations with men, since she does not speak Arabic. Yet she is most often touched by the way women, seeming to sense her pain, take her into their homes and lives.

Loss threads through Gunn's life, making her sense of homecoming among the Palestinian families of Deheishe poignant and her concern for them understandable. Evoking memories of girlhood—the loss of her father, the frightening experience of a sudden emptiness in the supposedly solid ground of her side yard—she moves to her broken marriage and her mother's death to make us see that she is a person seeking to know how to survive loss. The circumstances that bring her to know Palestine as more than a biblical place or the home of "terrorists" are related to this search: it was on a sabbatical spent in Israel studying autobiographical writing of Holocaust survivors that she first went to the West Bank.

Gunn's perspective as someone who worked with the Palestinians determined not only the form in which she chose to write this memoir (as a counterbalancing "discourse of familiarity") but also the very possibility of knowing the details of everyday life that make such writing possible. Only if you sit in the hospital and see the injury cases coming in can you know what the Intifada meant to those who were punished. Only if you stay in the homes of Deheishe, once tents and now of concrete block, can you know what it is like to live the curfews, searches, and violence that are the "security measures" of the Israeli state.

Her description of the mundane realities of curfew from the perspective of its objects is revealing. We in the United States read about curfews in the newspapers, and the view is always from the outside—from the point of view of those who impose the curfew. How often do we think what it means for those who are confined, unable to go out or to get supplies? Gunn tells us of boredom. Curfew from the inside, Gunn says, is about "numberless cups of sweet tea, long hours of American sitcoms and Egyptian melodrama on television, and endless watching of the criss-crossing army patrols and groups of youths." After a few days, "even the sound of live ammunition [becomes] an unremarkable part of the background noise."

Gunn's view of Israelis is also determined by her situation. She encounters them as soldiers in her visits to the refugee camp and as officials in her efforts to get medical care and protection for her teenage friend. They shine flashlights in her face and ask where she is going; they knock on the door and search the house she is staying in; they carry guns and shoot people. They display large Israeli flags when they know it will be most offensive. She talks to them in English as a weapon to protect herself and her friends. She is met with surprise, sometimes hostility. Occasionally there is inexplicable politeness or a fleeting moment of common humanity. She notes their occasional fear and embarrassment; more commonly she notes their arrogance or that terrible declaration that "I'm only doing my job." This is a situated, embodied view of Israelis; it is what they look and feel like when you are in a region under military occupation, in a Palestinian camp that would not be home to 1,650 families unless they had been forced out of their villages and towns, first in 1948 and then in 1967.

For writing and talking about the Middle East, people usually invoke the ideal of "balance" rather than "objectivity." Yet if one looks closely, one sees that the requirement of balance is enforced only selectively. It applies only to those who are perceived to *have* a perspective: those, in other words, who are differently situated from the dominant, with their perspectiveless perspective. Above all, it applies to those who are situated to know the Palestinian experience. In following Donna Haraway's argument, however, it is precisely Janet Varner Gunn's *situatedness* that gives her knowledge its weight.

Giving Voice

Gunn fears that her desire to give voice to the Palestinian people she lived among might have been subverted by her writing this memoir, by the educated Western outsider again speaking for others. But her story of the failure of her autobiography workshop for the Palestine Human Rights Information Center reminds us why outsiders are still needed to *give* voice.

As a Human Rights Center volunteer, she was assigned the task of producing a report on the martyrs of the Intifada, the victims of Israeli state violence. She decided that instead of documenting the circumstances of their deaths, horrifying but numbing, she wanted to profile their lives. It was, after all, as she shows so clearly in *Second Life*, the courage of these young men and women that was celebrated in Palestinian homes, schools, and public events.

Rather than writing the profiles herself, however, she wanted to train the Palestinian field-workers at the center, those who knew the families and the community, to do this writing. She tried to set up a workshop on autobiographical writing for them, but during her two years there she was never able to get the workshop going. Israeli curfews kept preventing meetings. And the Palestinian human rights workers who were supposed to attend the workshop kept disappearing, not because they were not interested, but because they had been taken into administrative detention and carried off for varying lengths of time to the crowded tents and scorching sun of Ansar III, where thousands of them would never be accused of anything specific or brought to trial. Because Palestinians are prevented in so many ways from speaking to the world, it is left to this woman scholar who found her way to the West Bank because she did not want to turn fifty in Greensboro, North Carolina, to give voice to some of them.

She need not worry about "confiscating" their story; by telling it she does not prevent Palestinians from also telling it, as they do through poetry, statements, actions, and even booklets like the 108-page political hagiography Gunn tells us the friends of her martyred "second son" have now written. But they tell it mostly to each other and in ways that sometimes need explaining to outsiders. Gunn is positioned to do that explaining. Calling this a project of border crossing, she offers the memoir as a path outsiders can take to cross over into Deheishe and learn something of how its people live and survive—and why they find it hard to accept the capitulations of "peace agreements."

Acknowledgments

My gratitude goes, first of all, to the Palestinian residents and friends of Deheishe Camp who made it possible for me to find more of my own story and then to write something of theirs. Many of them I name and give a place in this book; others, for a variety of reasons, remain outside of or unnamed in these pages but gave me the courage to write them.

My way to Deheishe was paved by East Jerusalem's Palestine Human Rights Information Center (PHRIC) and its director, Dr. Jan Abu-Shakrah, and also by Samir Abu-Shakrah, Jan's husband, whose love of philosophy, literature, and politics I found among so many of my Palestinian friends. Thanks also to PHRIC's field-workers, especially Mohammad, Simon, and Terry, who first told me about the seriously injured teenager who would become the center of this memoir.

To doctors, nurses, orderlies, and guards at Makassad Hospital where I first met the teenager, Mohammad Abu Aker, I want to say *shukran*. Makassad, as I will later describe this Palestinian institution on Jerusalem's Mount of Olives so important during the Intifada, became another home for me.

My special thanks to those who read or responded to readings from my book in its various stages: Hisham Ahmed, Ammiel Alcalay, Alan Anderson, Tim Buckley, , Barbara Crockett, Natasha Fairweather, Robert Fortna, Mary Gerhart, Beth Goldring, Nina Gregg, Lori Hasbrook,

Raymond Hicks, Diane Hitti, Biodun Iginla, Michael Lynk, Ina Macaulay, Ruth Mouly, Maya Rosenfeld, Robert Sayre, Barbara Schumann, Albert Stone, Kevin Thomas, Louise Beckley Varner, Anita Vitullo, and Joanne Waghorne.

Editorial assistant Elizabeth Knoll Stomberg superintended the book's publication from start to finish over the Pittsburgh-Grahamstown (South Africa)-Jerusalem electronic superhighway; copyeditor Lynn Marasco cleared out clutter, caught errors large and small, and read me like a book! Without them, nothing.

To Teo Savory, Alan Brilliant, and Donna Elliot Frick, I want to give another kind of thanks. They knew before I did how important it was for me to leave school even though (maybe because) school had been home for half a lifetime—from the year my father died to the year I became a university department chair. In helping me make the break with school, they helped me reconnect with my life.

Finally, I am indebted to the two sons who enabled my border crossings and to whom I dedicate this book.

Prologue

An Autobiographical Experiment

As I'm not an archivist or a historian or anything like it, I'll only have
spoken of my life to tell the story, a story, of the Palestinians.
—Jean Genet, *Prisoner of Love*

Until I began a research year in Israel in the fall of 1986, Palestine was for
me the name of an ancient land I had studied in Old Testament courses
back in the late fifties. I was born in the year that marked the beginning
of the Palestinians' first Intifada, but it would take nearly another fifty
years before our respective lives began to intersect in their second uprising. Until then, twentieth-century Palestine was off my map except as the
site of bearded terrorists.

Jean Genet's story of the Palestinians began in the early seventies at the
height of fedayeen activity in Jordan. Genet had arranged for a few days'
visit to a Palestinian military encampment and ended up spending nearly
two years with the young fighters he describes in his posthumously published memoir, *Prisoner of Love*. My story begins in the second year of
the recent Palestinian uprising and covers two years in the life of one of
its martyrs, Mohammad Abu Aker, a teenager who was critically shot
during a stone-throwing demonstration in his refugee camp in early August 1988. Mohammad managed to stay alive for two years following his
injury and then died of complications in October 1990. They were the
same two years during which I, too, was gaining a second life after a series of losses.

My story of both our second lives begins in the late summer of 1988,
when I took two years out of my teaching career to do human rights

work on the West Bank. Over the course of those two years, Palestinians moved into the center of my map and, indeed, began to transform it as I became involved with Mohammad, his family, and his camp. The routing to those years in Palestine took me through an earlier sojourn in Israel, where, in the academic year 1986-87, I spent a sabbatical to write a book on Holocaust autobiography. I, as my trade demands, had established my "scholarly credentials" on the genre of autobiography in a book I published in 1982.[1] In defining a theory of autobiography that I called a "poetics of experience," I wanted to situate the genre within the lived experience of historicity and temporality where "selving" is made possible, I argued, by the limits of finitude and the Other. To exceed those limits, I argued, was to drown in depth, the fate of Narcissus. Having in mind Holocaust writing like Saul Friedlander's *When Memory Comes* and Primo Levi's *Survival in Auschwitz*, I argued further that autobiography is a form of survival literature, a writing *for* one's life, not simply *about* it. Now a survivor of a broken marriage and the recent death of my mother, I felt ready to join a nation of greater survivors.

There was, to be sure, a less momentous reason for heading east: I can still remember coming to a red light on High Point Road one rainy afternoon in the early spring of 1986 and deciding I did not want to turn fifty in Greensboro, North Carolina. I had already applied for leave from the University of North Carolina, where I had been teaching since getting a Ph.D. at age forty. Europe seemed too close to home, the Third World too far away. I decided that Israel was a good place in between.

I knew little about Palestinians when I arrived in Israel, except for the unshaven face of Yasser Arafat and warnings from colleagues to stay clear of "Arabs" in Jerusalem's Old City, *Palestinians* being a term that came into general use only with the uprising (Intifada) a year later. Through friends in the States, I eventually met a woman who, like me, had been a graduate student at the University of Chicago and was working at the time in East Jerusalem for a Palestinian weekly newspaper published in English. Through Beth, I learned about a tour I thought safe enough to join since it was organized by an Israeli then living in London. I learned later that the organizer, Uri Davis, was persona non grata in Israel for his protest activity against Israeli policy in the Occupied Territories during the 1970s. The Jerusalem Peace Tour, as it was called, began inside Israel. The small group of us, all women, met with Palestinians—a journalist, a poet, and a resident in a village near Nazareth—who told us about government confiscation of village land and inequities in funding to Arab towns.

We also visited the site of a Palestinian-Christian village in the far north of the Galilee, destroyed except for its church. Israel had turned the area into a national park. We happened to meet an old woman, a former resident of the village, who was back picking wild garlic—a figure out of a Tolstoy novel, head covered with a triangular scarf, a long apron over her billowing skirt. When we invited her to get into our tour bus, she instead walked at an astonishing clip ahead of us—as it turned out, to retrieve a heavy carton of the garlic she had stowed away in the bushes.

We drove her to the nearby town of Jish, where she was now living with her grandson and his family. Through her grandson, Rashid, who spoke English, we learned the story of their former village, Kufr Bir'im. Its residents had agreed to vacate the village in 1948 during Israel's War of Independence, or what Palestinians call the Catastrophe (*Al-Nakba*), on assurances that they could move back "in fourteen days" as soon as the fighting was over. Those fourteen days stretched into forty more, during which time the village was destroyed except for the main sanctuary of the Maronite Christian church, to which they continued to return for Christmas and Easter services and weddings among the roughly fifteen hundred people who made up the current village population. Ever since they had to leave, the village council-in-exile had been sending a yearly letter to the Ministry of the Interior to remind Israel of its promise of return. In the meantime, the old men and women like Rashid's grandmother hitch rides back to the village site to pick grape leaves, collect basil, and tend to the secretly established tomato garden while enjoying the breeze and listening to the stillness.

By far the most moving part of the tour took place in Jabaliya, a Gaza refugee camp of 67,000. I will never forget the dignity with which we were received into the hovels that have been described as the Soweto of the Middle East. According to the Israeli and American social scientists Meron Benvenisti and Sara Roy, the area had been "de-developed" by Israel since it took over administration of Gaza from Egypt in 1967. Little wonder it should be that piece of occupied territory Israel was first willing to give up along with Jericho in the fall 1993 round of secret peace talks in Oslo. What was so striking about my visit, however, was the absence of a "culture" of poverty. In the middle of degrading circumstances, the Palestinians we met in Jabaliya refused to be degraded.

It was shortly after that February 1987 tour that I put my Holocaust project on the shelf and began my first round of volunteer human rights work at East Jerusalem's Arab Studies Society, editing a report on the uprooting of olive trees in a West Bank village. I returned to the society's human rights center two years later, after resigning my tenured position in religious studies in North Carolina. Having sat out the U.S. civil rights movement and the Vietnam War protest during the sixties, I joined my first cause in the late eighties, a middle-aged academic on the other side of the world.

Had I gone to the West Bank much earlier than the summer of 1988, I would have been oblivious to some things and taken different notice of others. I would not yet have become the person to whom Mohammad Abu Aker's mother said, as she did one evening in the family's glass-enclosed veranda, "You have been running until you reached Deheishe Camp." My life would not yet have prepared me for that evening nor for most of the rest of what I found when I did finally reach Deheishe Refugee Camp.

Deheishe, the primary setting of my book, is one of sixteen refugee camps on the West Bank. Located near Bethlehem on the main road between Hebron and Jerusalem, the camp has a signature twenty-foot-high fence that runs its entire length. The first part of the fence was erected by the Israeli military government in 1985 and was then extended in several stages in a vain effort to protect Israeli settlers' cars on the road side of the fence from stone-throwing Palestinian youth inside.

My two-year involvement with Mohammad, first with his "case," then with his life, opened the door to Deheishe and its nearly eight thousand residents. The camp provided a good look at the Intifada, which began in late 1987 and continued as the September 1993 Oslo Accords ("Gaza-Jericho First") were being attacked on both Israeli and Palestinian sides. The word *intifada* means a shaking off like the movement of a wet dog, but the uprising that began in late 1987 went much deeper than that. Far more than a shaking off of a surface irritation, the Palestinians' struggle for self-determination goes all the way down to fundamental questions about how a people will live its daily life. How will they educate their children when schools and universities are closed? Where will they sleep when their houses are sealed or demolished? How will they plan for their collective needs when public gatherings are outlawed? What will they plant in their fields and gardens when even certain flowers are on the forbidden list? Even more fundamental than these questions is the one about how they will think of themselves as a people.

Until a flashpoint was reached in early December 1987, most Palestinians had seemingly learned to accommodate themselves to life under occupation. Movement controlled by checkpoints, official organizing limited by military law, planting dictated by long lists of prohibitions—these and hundreds of other regulations had become business as usual. After twenty years, occupation was a way of life.

During its first phase, the Intifada not only brought unprecedented unity among Palestinians but also succeeded in dispelling any illusion that they could somehow manage to live under occupation without paying too high a price. A civil revolution, the Intifada was, first of all, a set of pervasive interventions into the mind-set of normalcy. As a first act of intervention devised by its local leadership, Palestinian businesses were to open for only half a day. They were asked to stay closed completely on frequently called general strike days, when, on the anniversary dates of certain historical events, the population was called upon to demonstrate solidarity against the 1979 Camp David Accords, about which the Palestinians had had no say, or the 1917 Balfour Agreement, in which the Jews were promised a homeland in Palestine by the British Mandate government. Boycotting of Israeli products and tax revolts like the one undertaken by the residents of Beit Sahour, a village near Bethlehem, represented other tactics of intervention that were meant to remind Palestinians of the economic dependence on Israel many had reconciled themselves to living with for more than twenty years.

Even the category of time itself was seized upon as an opportunity for intervention when the Intifada leadership declared that Palestinians would set their own dates for beginning and ending daylight savings time. That decision did not go unnoticed by Occupation authorities: Soldiers beat scores of youths whose watches, which the soldiers usually smashed, were set to their own time.

But the real revolution was happening not on the streets but in the minds of Palestinians themselves when, equipped with renewed notice of the structures of oppression under which they had been living since 1967, they began moving beyond accommodation. Taking clear notice of these structures was the first stage in their liberation struggle. It was, in fact, the stage most threatening to the Occupation: The soldier in Gaza, as I will be reporting later, was not giving in to gratuitous cruelty when he shot a caged song sparrow on his way out of a Khan Yunis house. The fact is that he could not risk leaving the bird alive to continue its song.

The accommodating population, however, had never included in its number most of the Palestinians living in refugee camps like Deheishe. While many residents of the towns and some of the villages had reached a modus vivendi with life under occupation, the camps had continued to raise a never-ending fuss. Most of them had refused the normalizing programs jointly sponsored by Israel and Jordan and partially financed by the United States in the 1970s. Installing modern sewage systems and replacing leaking roofs were no acceptable substitute for self-determination. Raw sewage and leaking roofs, like the chain-link fence erected the length of Deheishe Camp, were badges of steadfastness (*sumud*). That the Intifada began in Gaza's Jabaliya Camp was no accident. That it then leapfrogged to the West Bank's Balatta Camp (Nablus region) was no surprise. The rest of the population ever since has been catching up to the resistance fervor that has defined the camps since 1967.

In the following pages, I mostly pay attention to particular faces and actions, trying to develop what Palestinian-American anthropologist Lila Abu-Lughod has called a "discourse of familiarity" that communicates how

> others live as we perceive ourselves living—not as automatons programmed according to "cultural" rules or acting out social roles, but as people going through life wondering what they should do, making mistakes, being opinionated, vacillating, trying to make themselves look good, enduring tragic personal losses, enjoying others, and finding moments of laughter.[2]

Deheishe people, in fact, love to laugh. It has been laughter, I think, that has helped them and their forebears live with dignity under so many years of occupation: first under the Turks, then the British and the Jordanians, and now the Israelis. "This is our situation; this is our life," they say again and again, not with resignation but with tragicomic realism.

At the same time, Deheishe is a camp of strugglers. My account of Deheishe will feature many of them, both women and men, old and young. As I will repeatedly observe, struggle and resistance have become for them second nature, the what-goes-without-saying that constitutes what French sociologist Pierre Bourdieu calls "practical knowledge" or "habitus."[3] While they insist on *living* their lives, they are also prepared to die for their rights. It is this combination that makes laughter come easily in Deheishe. Despite the fact that they have no political rights and their human rights are daily violated, Deheishe residents are among the most liberated people I know.

I will be turning to the struggle and the laughter and sometimes the tears in the pages ahead. For now, I want to talk about the autobiographical dimension of this book. Its subject matter came out of my own experience and represents what I myself was in a position to see and hear. With no effort at offering a balanced account of a situation that, after all, lacks symmetry, I tell the Deheishe story through my own "I" because I cannot imagine telling it in any other way. It was through the horizon of my own experience that I had access to the landscape of Deheishe. What was normal to its residents was often strange to me, but that very fact ensured that I would notice it. Home invasions, for example: I was on the scene five of the times that army patrols entered Mohammad's house, but the last time was as shocking to me as the first even though such experiences were an unexceptional part of Deheishe's daily round.

Over the course of the two years I lived half my life in the camp, I had to find ways to adjust my horizon of expectations in order to help steady my nerves. To keep noticing, to keep being startled was far too wearing. So I, too, learned to laugh instead of shudder. The enormity of the outrage under which Deheishe lived its ordinary life hit me full force only when I left Palestine for the familiar territory of home.

Not only did I get to the Deheishe story by way of my own, it was also the other way around: I came to myself by way of Deheishe. In addition to the frame of acceptance I brought with me, I discovered more of my life story while I was there. Mohammad's mother was dead right: I *had* been running until I reached Deheishe. Those two years uncovered much of what I was running from. One of the clues had been in front of me from the beginning, in a photograph of myself as a little girl I had brought along with me to the West Bank. With Mohammad's mother's words fresh in my mind, I described that photograph in my journal after returning to my East Jerusalem apartment the morning after the evening on the veranda:

> I see a little girl standing next to a round wooden table on which there is a stuffed dog. The little girl is looking slightly to the left while her body is turned slightly to the right. She and the stuffed dog are facing in the same direction, off toward some object beyond the camera's eye. It is impossible to know what her eyes are registering. They are opened wide but, together with her mouth which refuses to smile, they suggest fear or, at least, a deep tentativeness. She wants to see, but she is not ready to take in what may be there. The little girl looks away from something, avoiding the camera's eye.
>
> She's wearing a short-sleeved cotton dress with a ruffle around the collar and sleeves. Sepia-toned, the photograph does not say what color

the dress is. It seems to match her high-tied shoes and short socks. I notice only now that she has something in her hands which she holds at waist level in front of her. It is her right hand that holds it, between her thumb which is on top and her fingers under it. The index and small fingers of her left hand point down loosely while the middle fingers curve under the object. She seems to be using that hand to cover the object more than to hold it.

Her hair is parted in the middle, its curls the result of bobby-pinned ringlets set the night before. Her right ear is exposed, strands of hair that escaped the bobby pins sticking out behind it. Not at home in the studio, there is little readiness in her expression. She is, in fact, not really present. "Tentative" is the word that describes her: her stance, her wide-eyed stare. Her hands are the only deliberate part of her. She is holding on and holding back, as though the undefinable object in her hands is the only thing that keeps her in place. It keeps her from floating off into space. It and the stuffed dog provide her gravity.

Some months after describing my photograph, I associated it with my father's dying nearly fifty years before. It took a particular childhood memory to make the connection between the photograph and my father. Once I recovered the memory, I realized something about why I had run to Deheishe. The memory came back to me in the course of setting up a workshop in autobiographical writing for Palestinian field-workers in the human rights center. Early on I had been assigned by the center's director to produce a special report on the martyrs of the Intifada, and I soon decided that the report should profile the *lives* of the martyrs and not simply put forward the circumstances of their deaths. I decided further that this profiling ought to be done by the Palestinian field-workers familiar with the lives of the martyrs rather than by an outsider like me. To better prepare them for the writing of these biographical sketches, I wanted to introduce the field-workers to ways of thinking about their own lives. One of the first writing assignments was to be a memory from their childhood.

As it turned out, we were unsuccessful in getting the workshop going because of scheduling problems caused by curfews that regularly kept field-workers from getting to work and by administrative detentions that kept them, one after another, in the huge tent prison, Ansar III, that Israel had set up in the Negev Desert at the beginning of the Intifada.

I decided to try out that first assignment myself, however, and wrote the following memory. Like the little girl in the photograph, I had then felt myself in danger of getting lost in space:

My father must still have been alive, so I would have been less than six. It may have been during those last months when he was dying upstairs in bed. I figure this because it was to my grandmother that I ran in panic when the hole suddenly opened up. She was still living in her house half-way down the block on Jefferson Avenue, the same street where I lived. I had run that half-block to reach her. Had my father been dead, she would have been living with me and my mother, because she moved in with us after my father and my grandfather died within two months of each other.

I think that both my father and "Da-dat" were dying when I decided to dig down to China in the little strip of ground between our property and the Bozichs' next door. I think I was wearing my slate-blue winter coat. It might well have been spring, but temperatures can stay in the 30s as late as mid-April in Western Pennsylvania. The ground wasn't frozen, but it was hard. I know that because I bent the large tablespoon I took out of the kitchen drawer to dig with.

I knew I could get to China if I dug deep enough. My second cousin, Roger, and I had tried to dig through to the other side of the world at the bottom of my yard the year before. We had dragged cinder blocks from the little factory across the alley, the kind I used for playing house with my hollyhock dolls. The blocks had arched holes in them, miniatures of the Arab-style room with its vaulted ceiling where I am writing down this memory. My cousin and I planned to use the blocks, and some old boards we found against the Seases' fence, to build scaffolding as we dug our way to China. We must have heard about local mine cave-ins, and we wanted our tunnel to hold.

So I knew about China when I started to dig that morning. And I knew it was very quiet and I thought I wanted to make something happen. I don't know how long I forced the spoon into the hard ground. I couldn't have dug more than several inches when the spoon suddenly dropped down. When I reached to recover it, I found nothing but a cavernous hole. It was then that I ran to my grandmother's house.

When I reached the bottom of Jefferson Avenue, I buried my face in my grandmother's lap. The musky smell of her apron momentarily shielded me from the terrifying knowledge of the emptiness that lay just below the surface of things.

Like the little girl, I too needed to make my way to the other side of the world some forty-five years later. Unlike the little girl, I was able to make it all the way through. But Deheishe Camp was the key to the tunneling. Fear of getting lost in empty space could be put aside in the steadfastness I found among people whose holding on to day-to-day lives was the "very content" of their struggle.[4] To get from my side yard to Deheishe Camp took most of my life, even though it seemed no distance at all when I finally got there. Mohammad's mother was right: I had been running all the while in her direction.

Several months before I left the West Bank to resume my teaching career in the United States, I happened to attend a U.S. performance of *Seeing Double*, playing one afternoon in early March at the Palestinian Al-Hakawati Theater in East Jerusalem. I caught the performance only because I ran into a North Carolina friend who was visiting the Occupied Territories on his way home from Egypt. The East Jerusalem performance of *Seeing Double* was unscheduled and, in fact, unauthorized by the Israel Festival, which had sponsored the American troupe's gig in West Jerusalem the night before. My friend had seen the play on the other side of town, and when I met up with him he was on his way to the Al-Hakawati performance to see how it would go over with a Palestinian audience. I tagged along.

Staged by the visiting San Francisco Mime Troupe, *Seeing Double* was about two young men from San Francisco, a Palestinian and a Jew, who go off to the West Bank to lay claim to the same piece of land. The American Palestinian, Salim Razali, is delegated by his family to take the Ottoman deed that will prove their ownership of property that is about to be confiscated for Jewish settlement. The American Jew, the "born-again" David Goldberg, has decided to make aliyah on the same piece of land, for which he has established biblical proof of Jewish ownership by means of a computer program.

The two young men travel on the same plane, which crashes in Israel. Their passports and briefcases having been switched, they proceed to undergo the comic confusion of being taken for one another by the respective relatives and officials who are waiting for them. The comedy is heightened by the fact that the two characters are played by a single actor who switches back and forth between Salim and David by means of simple props: a pair of drumsticks for Salim, who has his own rock group in California, and a pair of horn-rimmed glasses for the more intellectual David. Others in the cast also have dual roles, both Palestinian and Jewish. One of the male actors plays the Rabbi Kahane-style rabid nationalist settler as well as the Arab terrorist, each of them itching to blow up the other's property. The only actors in single roles are those playing the Israeli soldiers, although two of them also play bass and drums for the musical accompaniment to the lively songs that punctuate the performance.

The comedy reaches a serious, even poignant, ending with news of a death in the house demolition that takes place in the farcical melee of an accidental detonation. Whether it is the death of Salim or of David is left unresolved, as their two mothers take opposite ends of the stage in mournful song and are then joined by the rest of the cast to sing about taking the "hand from the other side": "This is the year of possibility," they sang, the time to "stop the downward slide."

Though set largely on the West Bank (or Judea-Samaria, according to David), *Seeing Double* is framed by America, where the performance begins and ends. It is America that fuels its energy and supplies its music and good fun. It is America that gives the performance its polish. It is also America that sings its heart out with a solution that begins with a handshake, much like the one between another Arab and Jew that would be staged some three years later by yet another set of Americans, directed this time by a new president, on the White House lawn.

Palestinian and Jew are finally the same person and share the same history. Only a set of incidental props distinguishes the one from the other. Both, after all, have families who love them and want only the best for them. Both have set out on a journey to recover their homeland. It is only extremists on both sides, themselves differing in nothing but dress, who stand in the way of friendship and trust.

The afternoon program ended with a line that the young man who played the dual role of Salim and David delivered: "Peace is the most important issue facing the world today, because no person can reach his or her potential without it." Spoken during the final question-and-answer period with the audience, the line turned out to be the afternoon's bottom line. Peace, it would seem, is finally a personal issue. It is a matter of stripping away the accidents of history and politics, readjusting one's perceptions, and joining the chorus line. America has the last word.

I was not surprised when my friend told me that the Palestinian audience that afternoon was far less responsive than the Israelis had been the night before. "California dreamin' " has little place on the Palestinian agenda. The human potential movement that shapes the message of *Seeing Double* is, in fact, an almost-perfect distortion of Palestinian aspirations for self-determination. While the former drives toward such personal fulfillment as will insulate the individual from the need for (and the needs of) others, Palestinian aspirations drive toward such political freedom as will enable effective solidarity for collective action: "People are people through other people," as a South African Xhosa proverb has it.

My own reaction to the performance was mixed. Not only did the play's reductive personalizing make me angry, it also made me nervous about using my own autobiography to tell a story about Palestinians. I too risked reducing their story to the personal history I had brought with me. But the story I wanted to tell was a story of lived experience, not an account of transcendent truth—a story of intersecting personal and political experience on both sides and of a double vision that was noncollapsible. Like Jean Genet, I was neither an archivist nor a historian. Nor, indeed, was I a journalist whose reports were meant to stand on their own. Access to these lives came from my Western Pennsylvania sense of location as well as from the West Bank, my side yard on Jefferson Avenue as well as the veranda in Deheishe Camp. How the view from my own life both opened up and closed off Palestinian lives was part of the story I wanted to tell.

Sometimes I felt myself neither here nor there, swamped by unattachable emotions or simply numbed by shocking events. At other times, I felt part of a chorus that, after suitably lamenting Palestinian suffering, could whisk itself off the stage with the flash of an American passport. It was keeping a journal that helped me through the difficult times, a survival strategy I had first turned to in earnest in the summer of 1974, when I moved from Chicago to Chapel Hill with my then husband and our young son. Leaving the flat plain of the Middle West, I found myself once again in the Back Country, its low mountains chaining down from the Western Pennsylvania Alleghenies where I grew up to the Carolina Piedmont where I would be living for the next twelve years, until, divorced, I would be going for the first time to Jerusalem, a city among other hills. Our son had just turned five when we left Chicago, and I found myself living once again the death of my father when I was about the same age.

During that year of transition, I planned a book about growing up in Western Pennsylvania and used my journal to write down what I could remember about my childhood, especially about my great aunts, maiden ladies who had made their way, all three of them, beyond the Alleghenies: for Aunt Mary's cultural summers at Lake Chautauqua, Aunt Clara's teaching in Williamsport, and Aunt Adah's nursing career in Philadelphia. In their respective retirements back to Portage, they would be competing for my grandmother's attention around our Sunday-noon dinner table, Aunt Adah commenting on the "splendid" gravy, Aunt Mary looking dour with her ill-fitting dentures, Aunt Clara maintaining the "dignified" silence that would be broken only by the demented profanity she shouted during her last weeks of life.

But instead of writing my own autobiography, I returned to school at the end of the first year in Chapel Hill to write a dissertation about the autobiographical writing of others. I have been led back to my own life by the more recent years with the Palestinians of Deheishe Camp. What I have finally written of it has been enabled by the experiences I shared with them.

It is already clear that I have transferred portions of my journal to these pages with only minor changes. Other entries I have incorporated into longer accounts, adding background and further details, which I hope will help my readers cross the distance between their lives and the ones I write about. Instead of a continuing narrative, I have presented these lives in a series of stories and vignettes that more accurately communicate the way they came to my attention. The ongoing story of Mohammad's second life holds together the sections of Part I, just as it helped hold together his family and friends in Deheishe during the two years he managed to stay alive. Part II is written in three longer sections that are organized around three of five returns I made to Deheishe after coming back to the United States in the summer of 1990. This second part begins with Mohammad's death in October 1990, continues with my post-Gulf War visit in June 1991, and ends with the opening of Middle East peace talks in Madrid the following October.

In using the genre of memoir to translate my experience of the Palestinian Intifada, I find myself obliged to address the questions that confront any Western portrayal of a Third World situation—particularly a portrayal that, like mine, is the end result of autobiographical reflection and represents the intersection of personal and political history. I address this set of issues in questions I asked myself on the occasion of the first anniversary of my return to Jerusalem. Again, I took up my journal to write about what happened that day:

Yesterday marked the first-year anniversary of my return to Jerusalem. I spent it on the beach in Herzliyya. I couldn't wait to get back in the car and head home.

Our commute to the beach, from East Jerusalem through Tel Aviv, had taken only an hour, but it covered (and covered up) centuries. Faster than the speed of sound, we went from antique hillsides outside Jerusalem to the prefab industrial buildings near Tel Aviv. The acres of Jewish settlements made palpable the most recent twenty years. Nothing, however, memorialized the three Arab villages in the Latrun region that had been destroyed in 1967.

The part of the town near the beach looked like Sarasota, Florida, a transplant of America into the Middle East. Is the memoir I am writing as unnatural a transplant? Is it, too, a means of muting other voices and superimposing myself on a landscape that belongs to others?

And then there was the beach and the sea, another of those large, undefined spaces like the Outer Banks off the coast of North Carolina where I felt agoraphobic some ten years ago when I camped there overnight. To be sure, I could look behind me on Herzliyya beach to see some landmarks, unlike the flat horizon on Ocracoke Island. I could see, for example, an old, now empty mosque. But that made me even more uncomfortable.

We saw only two Palestinians that afternoon among the Israelis and the Westerners like ourselves. They were the two boys who cleared the beach of garbage. I spoke to them when we left and was able to find out they came from Nablus, easily two hours away through territory that is especially hostile these days.

Herzliyya beach was more than a moon-landing for me. It was also a time-capsule, overcrowded with forty years of my own history: sun-bathing at the public pool in Western Pennsylvania, living among the palmettos and banyan trees in Florida, hyperventilating on the empty dunes of Ocracoke, and, less than a week ago, being led by Joffer through the dense warrens of Deheishe Refugee Camp. Am I, too, expropriating Palestine to construct my own sense of place?

That unsettling thought, the possibility of confiscating the Palestinian story to establish my own, haunts my entire project.

I could have written about the Big News: deaths, injuries, collective punishments, detentions, beatings, house demolitions, land confiscations. Some of that breaks into my narrative, but I was more interested in the Small News about ordinary life: about the Gazan woman's marketing during a clash, about the sister-in-law's continuing to cross-stitch during a house invasion, about Anwar's finding a way of staying in a game of marbles. Not so much the horror stories but the accounts of ongoing and often tacit resistance built into daily life: these are the experiences I chose to write about.

I could have written about the bad soldiers who patrolled the camp. "Abu Negro," as camp residents nicknamed him for his Afro hairstyle, was legendary among the residents for his gratuitous cruelty. But I myself never saw the man. Instead I saw men whose stiff faces failed to hide their fear and embarrassment at what they were doing, although it would not have surprised me to see them beating up women and children or even taking aim and shooting one of the youths. While these things were normal for the camp residents, they never happened in my presence, probably *because of* my presence. Whatever the case, I saw the Israeli soldiers as themselves victims of the Occupation.

This is a book about human experience and human relationships unusually full of passion. It is a book that fleshes out my own humanity as well as the humanity of Mohammad and the people of Deheishe whom Western media represent as rejectionists, radical extremists on the left, and terrorists. Facts alone turn cold on the page without some sense of the life out of which they come. It is this sense of life I want most of all to communicate, hoping that my readers will be moved not by the victimization of an oppressive occupation but by the examples of hope and steadfastness I discovered in Deheishe's holding on for dear life. I want my readers to be struck by the persistent and inventive "mechanisms of survival" by which the people of Deheishe have insisted on living their lives—indeed, to acknowledge how increasingly critical is such survivor knowledge in a world typified by Sarajevo, Los Angeles, and, more recently, Hebron.[5] As an outsider, I was hesitant to write a formal human rights report about Palestinian martyrs whose lives I did not know. Instead I have written a first-person account of a young martyr whose second life became entwined with my own. My part in keeping him alive turned out to be a gift to myself as much as to his family and friends in Deheishe. Mohammad gave many of us our second lives.

Shortly after the first anniversary of Mohammad's death, I learned that the camp was writing its own story of Mohammad. In his transatlantic phone call to announce its publication, Mohammad's older brother told me that the monograph, made up of contributions from many residents, was part of Deheishe's continuing struggle. "It is our new experiment," Nidal said. I offer this book as yet another experiment.

PART I

A SECOND LIFE

Chapter 1

The "Living Martyr"

I first met Mohammad Abu Aker at an Arab hospital on Jerusalem's Mount of Olives in late August 1988, about a month after I had arrived on the West Bank to begin two years of Palestinian human rights work. The sixteen-year-old teenager had been critically injured on the morning of August 6 when, during a stone-throwing demonstration in his refugee camp near Bethlehem, a soldier shot him in the lower abdomen with the kind of high-velocity bullet that fragments on impact. For the previous eight months, Mohammad had been on the wanted list for his resistance activity. On the run, he had slept outside the camp most nights, returning home from time to time to shower and get fresh clothes.

According to eyewitnesses, the soldier had taken aim from a nearby rooftop that August morning. As Mohammad fell, a second bullet narrowly missed his head. Women rushed out of their houses to surround him as the soldier raised his automatic rifle in both hands in a seeming gesture of victory. Friends managed to get him to a Bethlehem hospital and then to East Jerusalem's Makassad Hospital, which treats the most serious Intifada injuries. After four and a half hours of emergency surgery to remove the exploded fragments, to cut out five feet of the small bowel, which had been perforated in eighteen places, to perform a hemicolectomy, and finally to wash out the abdominal cavity, Mohammad was not expected to live.

At the insistence of his father, Mohammad underwent more surgery three weeks later to remove the necrotic material resulting from the onset of gangrene, which destroyed most of the rest of his small bowel. It was an effort, in the end, to make his body sweet for burial. The family had already ordered the picture posters that had by then become conventional trappings for Intifada martyrs' funerals. Except for Mohammad's mother, everyone had given up hope.

It was during preparation for this second surgical procedure that I put my head around the door of Makassad's intensive care unit to have my first (and I thought my last) look at Mohammad. A Palestinian field-worker at the human rights center had told me I should get to the hospital quickly, before the teenager became another story in the martyrs' reports I had been assigned to write for the Palestine Human Rights Information Center's monthly *Update* on human rights violations. I saw Mohammad for only a few minutes. He was skeletal and moaned with every breath he took.

But two weeks later, I was on my way back to Makassad Hospital for Mohammad's seventeenth-birthday celebration. Flowers were taped to the walls of his room and the last of the hundreds who had come that day were about to leave by the time I got there. I arrived at the hospital in the company of two small boys from Deheishe, Mohammad's refugee camp. One of them, Khalil, had insisted on paying my taxi fare from the Old City's Damascus Gate up to the hospital when they learned I was on my way to Mohammad's party. They had been visiting him regularly, sometimes walking part or all of the way from Bethlehem when they did not have money for a bus or taxi.

On the next of what were to become increasingly regular visits, I joined Mohammad's family for the hot meal they ate each afternoon on the balcony across from his room on the surgical floor. The first time I met his mother, I extended my sympathy, through the help of a translator, for the suffering Mohammad and the family had had to endure. His mother would have none of my concern. She reared up and said that her other sons might have to be shot, as this was the life they were living. "This," she said, "is 'Our Situation,' " a phrase—the equivalent of Northern Ireland's "Troubles"—I would be hearing regularly over the next two years. She went on to say, as though in answer to my surprise at her show of stern resolution, that she kept her sadness in her heart, not on her face. "But when I go home and see Mohammad's shoes," she ended, "I cry." The food, kept hot with blankets and delivered daily by camp youths, was for the family. With no intestines, Mohammad was surviving on in-travenous fluids and willpower.

A week or so after Mohammad's birthday, I met his surgeon, Khaled Qurie, and learned that the teenager's life depended on getting a small-bowel transplant in the West. I suggested to Dr. Qurie that we co-author a special report that might catch the attention of the outside medical world. But I knew by the time I left the hospital that the article would barely get written, let alone published, in time to save Mohammad. Down to ninety pounds by then, he was starving to death.

From the hospital, I took a taxi straight to the home of Jan Abu-Shakrah, the American director of East Jerusalem's Palestine Human Rights Information Center, where I was volunteering. I walked into her Beit Hanina apartment and announced that we had to do something im-mediately about Mohammad Abu Aker. She straightaway picked up the telephone and put through a transatlantic call to a Canadian, Professor James Graff, who taught philosophy and directed a foundation for Near East culture and education in Toronto. Jim, who is legally blind, had re-cently established a small network for bringing eye-injured Palestinian children to Canada for medical treatment. Jan made the call on Yom Kip-pur. Thirteen days later Mohammad was on his way to Boston's New En-gland Deaconess Hospital for lifesaving treatment. Given the daunting list of arrangements necessary to get a wanted person out of the country and into surgical hands that could perform the still-experimental trans-plant on the other side of the world, what happened so quickly was noth-ing short of a miracle.

First, there was the problem of finding a transplant program that could carry out the procedure. Only three U.S. hospitals—Chicago's Rush Presbyterian, University of Pittsburgh, and Boston's New England Deaconess—had any experience. The Chicago and Pittsburgh hospitals had each done one transplant on humans by that time, but both patients had died. Deaconess had successfully transplanted intestines, but only in animals.

Second, there was the problem of finding an airline willing to trans-port Mohammad. All U.S. carriers refused liability for such a serious case.

Third, there was the problem of money, to cover not only the trans-plant but also the costs of transportation. KLM finally agreed to trans-port him, but space equal to three banks of seats would be needed to ac-commodate his stretcher. Moreover, the Dutch airline could take him only as far as New York. A medical airbus, costing an additional $2,800, would have to get him from JFK to Logan Airport in Boston.

But there were the more immediate problems of getting him quickly out of Israel: finding a way to accelerate the long laissez-passer process for a travel document often refused to Palestinians; arranging for the Israeli ambulance service, Magen David, to transport Mohammad from Makassad to the airport, since the hospital's own ambulances would not be cleared by Ben-Gurion Airport security; getting the International Committee of the Red Cross (ICRC) to provide its own security for Mohammad, whose departure might well be aborted by his arrest since he was on the military's wanted list before he was shot.

Beyond those logistical, financial, and political problems was the moral problem raised by the U.S.-based Physicians for Human Rights. Under any cost-benefit analysis, Mohammad's case was questionable at best, since the large sum of money involved could be divided among so many others or spent on someone whose outcome was less risky. Moreover, as the group's Dr. John Constable of Massachusetts General Hospital pointed out, the treatment needed to ready Mohammad for the transplant procedure could take a considerable period of time during which his quality of life would be impaired. It would be better for Mohammad, he advised, to have the treatment in a "native culture" if at all possible. He advised against taking Mohammad to another part of the world until possibilities in Cairo and Amman had been checked out.

The complicated process on the U.S. end was moved forward by Louise Cainkar and Donald Wagner of Chicago's Palestine Human Rights Campaign. They were able to secure a pledge of $50,000 from a new Washington foundation set up for medical needs of Arabs in the United States as well as to work out travel logistics with an Arab-American travel agency in Chicago for the medical airbus company that would have to transport Mohammad from New York to Boston. Along with Jan and others, I worked on the West Bank and Israel end to facilitate the laissez-passer with the help of the center's connections with Knesset members Dedi Zucker and Yossi Sarid of the Meretz Party; to arrange for Mohammad's airport security with the Red Cross; and to tend to the other odds and ends of sending a dying refugee and his father on their first trip to the West.

For all of us, it was Jim Graff's memorandum to ICRC's Vienna headquarters that galvanized our efforts. "We are fully aware of the cost/benefit, risk/success issues involved," the Canadian professor wrote:

But our inclination is to do whatever we can to try to save the boy's life. . . . We know full well that the monies raised for this project could be spent to help many others who are in need of treatment which we can reasonably predict to be successful. We also realize, however, that monies raised for this project . . . might stimulate contributions for less dramatic projects, and that when everything is reckoned together, one cannot quantify . . . prognosis of success when dealing with human life. There is a time when it is fitting to focus on an individual human being, to take risks and to stretch our capacities to their limits. We think this is such a time.[1]

Having become so involved in Mohammad's case, I was asked to accompany him to Boston. We broke up the long trip in Amsterdam (where a Dutch woman hastily left the table at which we had joined her for coffee on learning Mohammad's father was an Arab) and then again at JFK in New York, where we had to leave behind several large pieces of luggage in order to fit ourselves and Mohammad, still on his stretcher, into the medical airbus that bobbed up and down through heavy rain to Boston. Sitting up front with the pilot, I kept my eyes closed except when I turned around to make eye contact with Mohammad's father, whose face was drenched with nervous perspiration.

The four of us—Mohammad, his father, his surgeon, and I—were greeted on that cold rainy night of October 4, 1988, by a small group of Palestinian and American well-wishers. Still strapped to a narrow gurney like the one he had lain on for the twenty-six-hour trip from Makassad Hospital, Mohammad somehow managed to smile and flash the V-for-victory sign from the ambulance waiting to rush him to Deaconess Hospital. He was wearing the Basque beret I had quickly taken off my head and put on his as he was being carried off the airbus. The *Boston Globe* carried the picture and story of his arrival the next morning, calling Mohammad a "living martyr."[2]

From the morning of Mohammad's arrival at New England Deaconess Hospital on that raw October night to his release three and a half months later, his regimen was to be full of machinery and testing—first, for adjusting and stepping up the intravenous feeding he had been getting over the past two months in Jerusalem and, second, evaluating him for a possible small-bowel transplant. With the loss of most of his small bowel, Mohammad had also lost the normal route of absorbing nutrients. In the short run, he needed an alternative system of nutritional support simply to keep him from dying. He would need a small-bowel transplant to keep him alive in the longer run.

On that first morning, Mohammad slowly walked up and down the corridor outside his private room attached to the dropper machine, which would be his steady companion for the next two years, after lying for two months in his Makassad Hospital bed. He and I joked about his strolling down what I called the "Salah ad-Din Corridor," Salah ad-Din being both the name of the main business street in East Jerusalem and the name of the celebrated Arab general (Saladin, as he came to be known) who defeated the Crusaders in 1187. Shortly after that first walk, highly trained specialists began their lifesaving work: the hospital's hyperalimentation team calculated the exact mixture of nutrients he needed. An enterostomal specialist decided how best to manage duodenal drainage so that his skin would stop drying out. A physical therapist started him on muscle-strengthening exercises. Three weeks later, he underwent surgery for the insertion of a permanent catheter into a major vein in his chest.[3] A week after that, he was discharged to a nearby hospital apartment for an additional two and a half months of outpatient care.

While medical specialists were saving Mohammad's life, I was taking care of transportation, financial, and communication problems. I made sure to have a supply of subway tokens on hand for daily trips that Mohammad's father, Dr. Qurie, and I took to the hospital from the apartment complex off Central Square where we were staying. In between endless cups of Arabic coffee at Algiers, a Palestinian-owned Cambridge coffeehouse, and daily McDonald's hamburgers in a little mall near the hospital, I found myself taking on the double roles of fund-raiser for an expensive medical case and public relations coordinator for a newsworthy political case. I soon bought an answering machine for the calls about Mohammad that began coming in from around the world.

In late October, Mohammad's father and I were featured speakers at a fund-raiser in Newark organized by Roots, a Palestinian cultural organization in Washington, D.C. Roots had helped arrange finances for Mohammad's medical treatment through the Naim Foundation, the organization recently established to meet the medical needs of visiting Arabs. Mohammad's father, also named Naim, joked that the foundation had been named for him. After we succeeded in raising $7,000 for the foundation from the relatively small group of Palestinian businessmen in the New Jersey area, we took the train back to Boston even though we had flown to Newark. Naim refused to board another airplane until he returned to the West Bank, at which point he would have no other choice. Obviously, he was still unnerved by our bumpy ride in the medical airbus from New York to Boston that rainy night several weeks before.

At another fund-raiser in Brooklyn, Mohammad's doctor and I raised an additional $5,000, part of which was put aside for our joint living expenses in Boston. In mid-December, just before I left Boston to help ensure Mohammad's safe reentry into Israel, I participated in a third fundraiser at the Algiers coffeehouse, which the owner had turned over for Mohammad's case.

My other role as public relations officer introduced me for the first time to Palestinian factionalism. Under self-imposed discipline on the West Bank and Gaza, the various political parties in the Occupied Territories were cooperating beneath the umbrella of the uprising's united leadership. In the East Jerusalem human rights center where I was writing reports on martyrs, Fatah, Popular Front, and Democratic Front supporters worked side by side. But factionalism operated in force among the young men and women living in the Boston area, most of whom had been born in refugee camps in Jordan and Lebanon and had never set foot in Palestine. Their imposed distance from the homeland and the added alienation of lives now being lived in a country whose foreign-aid largesse made possible more than twenty years of Israel's occupation of what they considered their homeland made especially sacred cows of their factional affiliations, largely Fatah, Yasser Arafat's mainstream party, and the Popular Front for the Liberation of Palestine, which stood to its left.

Whether or not suspicion characterized all of their relationships, it came to be evident in Mohammad's case. He was the first widely publicized Intifada victim to be brought to the United States. His Deheishe friend Maysoun Gerash had come to Chicago for medical treatment a month before he had arrived, but she had walked into the United States with a shattered elbow while Mohammad came in on a stretcher, nearly dead from starvation.[4] Following the *Boston Globe*'s depiction of Mohammad as a "living martyr," the political dimension of his case could not be ignored.

I became aware only in retrospect of factional competition over taking credit for Mohammad's Boston treatment, long after I had returned to the West Bank in late December. As it turned out, the Boston factions had been competing over Mohammad's case from the time they organized their welcome at Logan Airport that rainy night. Things came to a head when one of the factions tried to arrange a news conference at Mohammad's hospital bedside. When I learned that the conference had not been cleared through the hospital's public relations office, I called the Boston newspapers and television stations to cancel it. As I learned later on, it had been a group affiliated with the faction Mohammad himself supported, the Popular Front for the Liberation of Palestine (PFLP), that had tried to arrange the occasion.

I began to have second thoughts about the respect I had paid to hospital protocol when, two years later in the summer of 1990, Deaconess denied readmission to Mohammad because of his outstanding bill with them. To be sure, the Boston hospital had been willing to treat him once again in the fall of 1989 on the strength of promises that the new set of costs, along with a good-faith payment toward the old set, would be paid up front. But financial complications became even worse when this promised funding never materialized.

The only funding source I knew about in the fall of 1989 for Mohammad's second visit to Boston was a European professor who had long been a conduit for money and equipment for various medical and agricultural projects in the Occupied Territories. She took a special interest in Mohammad's case when she was visiting the West Bank in late February 1989, shortly after Mohammad had returned from his first trip to Boston. Meeting him while he was back again in Makassad Hospital, she bought him a color television and provided rent money for the Bethlehem apartment he would be using when Deheishe was under curfew or while its residents were being submitted to systematic house invasions by soldiers in search of wanted youth.

When it came time for Mohammad's next checkup, I was able to take him back to Deaconess Hospital on the strength of the professor's guarantee that $25,000 would be wired from a European city to Boston within a week of Mohammad's arrival. Dr. Anthony Sahyoun, one of the surgeons in charge of Mohammad's case, had projected costs amounting to $20,000 for the battery of tests, the replacement of the Hickman catheter, and the hyperalimentation Mohammad would need during his month-long visit. The other $5,000 would be a good-faith payment against the already existing bill of $50,000 beyond what the Naim Foundation had been willing to pay.

Mohammad and I arrived in Boston on August 28, 1989, for his second visit. I left for my thirty-fifth high school reunion in Western Pennsylvania four days later, after nutrition and testing arrangements were made with Deaconess Hospital and Mohammad was settled in the apartment of a young Palestinian couple and their infant daughter. Reading from an early version of this book back in North Carolina on September 9, I began a three-week speaking tour that would be taking me across the country and, as I had planned it, back to Massachusetts in time to rejoin Mohammad for our return flight to Tel Aviv on October 1. When the money had not arrived by September 6, I was on the telephone almost daily to Europe—from Greensboro; Bowling Green, Kentucky; Iowa City, Iowa; and, finally, Boulder, Colorado. Despite repeated assurances from my contact that money was on the way, it had not arrived in Boston by September 21, when I decided that Mohammad had to return to the West Bank on his own just to keep eating: Dr. Sahyoun insisted that the hospital could no longer absorb the cost of his $200-a-day hyperalimentation.

Months later, I heard vague rumors about a New York lawyer to whom a European bank might have sent the money. But the professor finally told me that the original source for the money, the Popular Front, had put a stop on the dispensing process pending additional proof of Mohammad's medical needs. It was not until the fall of 1993 that I learned that both of us, the professor and me, had been duped, possibly to embarrass the head of Washington-based Roots, Salah Tamari, to whom Dr. Sahyoun had once again turned when the promised funding never materialized. Having never received a promised wire from Cairo, Tamari, it seemed, was out of the loop.[5] Whatever the case, the Deaconess doors slammed shut on Mohammad.

Back in the fall of 1988, I was aware only of ruffled feathers that I attributed to growing frustration over the unfolding financial complications of Mohammad's case. By the time Mohammad died two years later, my education in Palestinian politics on the international scene was further along.

On Mohammad's first discharge from Deaconess Hospital in mid-January 1989, his weight was up to 108. He had been evaluated positively for a small-bowel transplant by a surgical team that included the Palestinian-American Anthony Sahyoun, who in 1946 had left Haifa, where his father was mayor, to study medicine in England. In addition, Mohammad had had a major surgical procedure, described in a Deaconess report as a "first stage small bowel transplant," to connect his duodenum and descending colon. But instead of proceeding further with the final transplant, Dr. Sahyoun decided to keep Mohammad on the program that the Deaconess hyperalimentation team had devised for him, at least until the transplant, still in its experimental stage, became less risky or until Mohammad's condition deteriorated to such a point that a transplant would be the only option. To give him a transplant then, Sahyoun had said to me, would be "like giving the boy AIDS." The antirejection drugs needed in such a massive transplant would so weaken his immune system that he could not stay alive long, especially back in a West Bank refugee camp.[6]

Over the course of those two and a half months of outpatient treatment, Mohammad's father was trained by the Deaconess hyperalimentation team to operate the dropper machine that infused liquid nutrition through a tube inserted into Mohammad's chest catheter. The chest site had to be kept sterile, and Naim was taught the elaborate cleaning procedure as well. Infection is endemic to hyperalimentation, as Mohammad would discover in the course of many spiking temperatures and regimens of antibiotics over the months ahead. Along with respiratory and kidney failure, it would lead to his death.[7]

In the January 12, 1989, discharge letter Dr. Sahyoun wrote to Mohammad's Makassad doctor, he indicated that Mohammad would need close and collaborative watching. If Mohammad's condition were to deteriorate, Sahyoun wanted him returned immediately to Boston. In the meantime, Sahyoun recommended regular six-month checkups, which turned out to be impossible to carry out under ongoing financial and political constraints.

I left Boston a month before Mohammad did to prepare for his safe return through Ben-Gurion Airport. Again, we had to be prepared for an attempted arrest as soon as he arrived. For all we knew, Mohammad was still on the wanted list. And since it would be Magen David, the Israeli ambulance service, that would be picking him up, we had to minimize the possibility of his being rerouted to an Israeli hospital where the military or Shin Bet could take him away for interrogation, as had happened in many other Palestinian medical cases.

For a second time, Knesset member Dedi Zucker was helpful. A young Israeli lawyer and a human rights worker associated with Zucker's political party (Meretz) were on hand at the airport along with two Israeli doctors, a Tel Aviv psychiatrist and an oncologist on the staff of Jerusalem's Haddassah Hospital, both of them members of Israeli-Palestinian Physicians for Human Rights. The psychiatrist, Dr. Ruhama Marton, was, in fact, the group's president. None of them seemed to think, as had crossed my mind, that we were playing out a John le Carré spy story.

The Jerusalem doctor began giving instructions to airport security police before the plane landed. "The boy will need immediate medical treatment," he told the officer in charge. "I want to be at his side as soon as he disembarks from the plane." The four Israelis, together with representatives from the Red Cross and the United Nations organization in charge of Palestinian refugee affairs, were ready to intervene on Mohammad's behalf at any sign of trouble.

Everything went smoothly except for what turned out to be a funny but slightly unsettling incident on the road out of the airport. Mohammad had been met with a wheelchair (although he was perfectly capable of walking) and was boarded into the Magen David ambulance. He was joined by his beaming mother, who had not been at all sure she would see Mohammad alive again when he left her three and a half months earlier. His father joined other family members in the car Mohammad's uncle had driven to the airport. I left with the Israeli doctor I had accompanied from Jerusalem, our vehicle third in the caravan leaving the airport.

On the way out of the area, Mohammad's father signaled the ambulance driver ahead of him to pull over so that he could join his wife and Mohammad. As he was walking toward the ambulance, he made use of traditional Arab nomenclature to introduce himself to its driver as the father of his oldest son: "I am Abu Nidal," he said. In not altogether mock horror, the Israeli driver reeled back, no doubt thinking of the infamous international terrorist who had broken away from the Palestine Liberation Organization (PLO). After a split second, the driver joined Mohammad's father in nervous laughter, and the Deheishe Abu Nidal climbed into the ambulance.

The rest of the drive back to Makassad was uneventful. Mohammad returned to his former room at the end of the surgical corridor, greeted along the way by the doctors, nurses, and orderlies who had helped keep him alive for the Boston treatment. Pictures and special messages were taped on the walls once again. The corridor outside his room became, as it was before he left for Boston, the reception area for scores of friends and foreigners who continued to make their pilgrimages to the site of the "living martyr." Many of the Deheishe comrades who had lined up during those first dark weeks to donate their blood and even to offer their intestines now came to celebrate Mohammad's return from the dead.

Mohammad had to stay in Makassad Hospital for an additional six weeks while open fistulas continued to drain and then were allowed to heal. It took most of that time to arrange for his homecoming at Deheishe

Camp, especially after what was called "Black Friday" in the Nablus area when the army had opened fire on a large funeral procession, killing eight of the mourners.[8] Any large gathering was at risk, and there were sure to be hundreds of people waiting in the street next to Mohammad's house. Once again, Meretz supporters and the ICRC had to be alerted, and their presence—along with that of the Israeli and international press—had to be made as visible as possible. The welcoming crowd would be seen from the military compound just across Hebron Road at the bottom of the steep hill from which Mohammad's house was in full view.

It was essential, too, for a United Nations representative to be part of the welcoming crowd, since that organization would have a continuing role in keeping Mohammad alive: its medical vans would deliver his weekly supply of nutritional bags and get him to the hospital when the camp was under curfew, and its international refugee affairs officers would intervene on his behalf at any sign of trouble from Israeli soldiers. Doctors in the camp's United Nations clinic would be on call for any ordinary medical problem that might come up.

After several delays in his discharge to get all the pieces in place, Mohammad came home again on March 6, 1989, to a shower of candy and flowers and women dancing in the street. It turned out that he was driven to the camp by Glenn Frankel, a Pulitzer Prize-winning *Washington Post* reporter whom I alerted to the occasion at the last minute. Frankel arrived at Makassad only minutes before Mohammad's discharge and ended up giving him and me a lift back to Deheishe. Frankel's feature story, "Wounds Transform Young Palestinian into a Legend," appeared in the March 8, 1989, issue of the *Washington Post* and was picked up by newspapers across the United States.

The homecoming celebration, which resembled nothing so much as the weddings that were a gala feature of Palestinian life before the Intifada, continued for three days. Hundreds greeted Mohammad as he emerged from Glenn Frankel's car. As Frankel wrote:

> Mostly they were children, many of them younger than 10, many in bare feet despite the afternoon chill. They choked the entryway to the house, strained for a glimpse of their frail hero and waited patiently on a winding reception line for a chance to shake his hand or kiss both cheeks.

The children's "devotion to Abu Aker and his legend," Frankel went on, "help[s] explain how the uprising is being kept alive, despite Israel's tough security crackdown." The journalist quotes a family friend: " 'All the children of Dehaishe [sic] know Mohammad's story. . . . When you see them playing in the alley-ways, they all want to be him.' "

Except for a momentary intrusion into the formal ceremony of hand-shaking and endless cups of tea and coffee that were served on the ground floor of the house, armed and helmeted soldiers kept their distance on a rooftop from which they could watch the coming and going of visiting delegations from the Bethlehem and Jerusalem regions. Camp youths, known as the Intifada *shabab*, or young male activists, stationed them-selves outside the walls of the Abu Aker compound. Among the outdoor crowd of well-wishers, Palestinian film director Michel Khalifeh was shooting footage for his project on the Intifada, which would be follow-ing *Wedding in Galilee*, a film shown in art cinemas around the world. Indoors, I was singing "You Are My Sunshine" to Mohammad; it was a favorite of my son when he was a toddler and the first song that came into my mind for such a happy occasion.

On the morning of the second day back at home, Mohammad walked through the camp to visit with the three families whose respective father and two sons had been martyred. On this formal visit of solidarity and condolence, Mohammad was accompanied by his father and older twin brothers, Nidal and Rafat. I was invited to go with them. The first visit was to the home of a thirty-five-year-old father of eight, Ibrahim Awad, who was shot in the head while he was sitting in his veranda. Although he had been killed on May 10, 1988, some months before Mohammad was injured, it was important for Mohammad, as a special kind of martyr himself, to visit the family once again. The second visit was to the family of fifteen-year-old Nabil al-Lawi, shot at close range on January 13, 1989, while carrying a supply of stones during a demonstration. Our last visit was to the house of Nazzem Abu Judeh, shot in the back of the head by a plastic bullet on October 1, 1988, and unconscious in the Makassad intensive care unit when Mohammad and I left for Boston. His mother had given me a silver pendant as I walked behind Mohammad's gurney that night, as though to send with us something of her son. Nine days later, I saw notice of his death in the October 12, 1988, issue of the *Boston Globe*, which carried the story of how four soldiers commandeered the red funeral van carrying his body after youths began throwing stones. The headline read, "Israeli troops seize body at funeral after some mourners hurl stones."

In the weeks and months that followed, Mohammad's whole family

learned how to operate the dropper machine on which his life now depended. Friends and neighbors helped carry in boxes of liquid nutrition
when United Nations made its weekly delivery. The entire camp went on
alert, watching for army patrols, when Mohammad eventually walked
out on his own into the pathways. When he was stopped by some soldiers
near his house, people were out of their houses within seconds to make
sure he was not ill-treated.

When, on another occasion, a patrol took him from his house for
questioning, residents lined the road all the way down to the camp fence
in order to take note of what was happening and to express their displea-
sure and concern. Keeping Mohammad alive became a national duty
both for Mohammad himself and for those closest to him.

When Mohammad died in the late fall of 1990, thousands from Deheishe
and surrounding communities broke a regional curfew to walk along
the mountain path behind his body to the nearby village of Irtas, where
he was buried in a small martyrs' cemetery. Reuters news service reported that there were more than three thousand people in the funeral
procession. As Mohammad's self-appointed archivist, his older brother
Nidal maintained a collection of medical reports, photographs, and
newspaper articles from around the world. A camp committee was soon
putting together a book to mark the first anniversary of Mohammad's
death.

It was as a "living martyr," an emblem of the Palestinian struggle that
itself had arisen out of its own ashes, that Mohammad Abu Aker became
a symbol of the Intifada. He had had the best slingshot, he had always
been at the front of demonstrations, he had remained strong under interrogation. But his life was no more remarkable than those of scores of others in the camp who had been active for many years, even before the Intifada. He was on the wanted list for eight months, but some of his
friends had been on it for much longer. His best friend, for example, had
been wanted for more than eighteen months before he was picked up.
Another friend had been on the wanted list for more than four years before he was arrested.

Nor was surviving an Israeli bullet enough for living martyrdom. One
wanted friend's twin brother, for years on and off wanted lists himself,
was shot three different times. Unlike Mohammad, Ya'coub was not
brought back from the dead. But one of his injuries, thought for a time to

have rendered him permanently sterile, was tantamount to a mortal wound.

Not just the fact that Mohammad was brought back from the dead, but the *timing* of that miracle made his case so special. Mohammad was shot in the ninth month of the Intifada and was returned to his people, alive and walking, about a month after the uprising's first anniversary. His life was being saved in Boston at the time that PLO chairman Yasser Arafat declared the independent state of Palestine in Algiers (November) and became its first president. The Madrid conference on Middle East peace opened a week after the first anniversary of Mohammad's death.

These coincidences were not lost on a people who had been so attentive to every detail of their history since 1948. Without a homeland of their own, such details, especially those involving martyrdom, became part of a history that Palestinians were making for themselves. That Mohammad was the first of a series of fallen warriors in one of the most politically active camps on the West Bank, that a young refugee had survived a "fatal" Zionist bullet in the ninth month of their historic uprising, that he was returning from the dead as the new state of Palestine was being born—these significant facts, fueled by longing and willed determination, took on mythic proportion for the people of Deheishe Camp and beyond. Mohammad had become a "revolutionary icon," as Israeli journalist Ori Nir had observed on visiting the teenager's hospital room, festooned with Palestinian posters and plaques, before he left for Boston.[9]

Mythmaking machinery went into operation from the moment Mohammad fell to the ground that August morning in 1988. The process was consolidated during three days of homecoming celebration when he was received like a bridegroom and at the close of which he made his ceremonial visits to the homes of fellow martyrs. At varying intensities, the machinery continued throughout his second life and in the account of his life as a struggler that was finally published in June 1992, too late for the anniversary for which it was planned but in time to commemorate the twenty-fifth anniversary of the Occupation. The 108-page political hagiography was written collaboratively by Mohammad's friends. Two photographs I took are among the eight that illustrate Mohammad's life from childhood through the carrying of his body to the grave site in Irtas. Both the front and back covers of the book feature Deheishe in its earliest days. A 1954 photograph of a large grouping of tents provides the back cover; on the front is a sketch of those tents on which is superimposed a triple image of a charcoal drawing of Mohammad's head and shoulders made for the occasion of his March 1989 homecoming. The publication is the first of its kind for an Intifada martyr.

No sooner was the account of Mohammad's life distributed among its residents than Deheishe Camp was experiencing the increasing demoralization of collaborators in its midst. At the same time, the Intifada was facing the potentially undermining prospect of ill-timed peace negotiations following the Gulf War, when Palestinians had fallen back into ignominy for supporting Saddam Hussein. Middle East talks began in Madrid under the Likud government and resumed in Washington under the new Labor government headed by Yitzhak Rabin, who, when he served as defense minister in Yitzhak Shamir's cabinet, introduced a policy that called for the breaking of Palestinians' bones.

A year after Mohammad's death, his brother Nidal hoped that events scheduled to celebrate the anniversary would help restore the camp's ebbing sense of solidarity and diminish its mounting sense of drift. Bethlehem military headquarters clamped a curfew on the camp that day, announcing it "in honor of" the martyr. The following day, there were a mere forty or so participants in a march through the mountains to Mohammad's grave in Irtas. To be sure, the camp was still under curfew, but only a year before more than three thousand participants had been willing to break a stronger curfew to join Mohammad's funeral demonstration.

Shortly before the second anniversary of Mohammad's death, his name was being invoked by two camp groups in disagreement over how the case of a suspected collaborator ought to be handled. Each side claimed the martyr's imprimatur as local and regional leaders were trying their best to avoid an open split within the party. Thanks to mediation efforts and, in no small measure, to the Israeli army, things came together for commemorating the anniversary. Anticipating that some kind of demonstration would be taking place inside Deheishe, the army imposed a curfew on the camp that morning, much as they had the year before. But the anniversary events took place outside the camp, at a Bethlehem location near the ICRC offices. It had been in front of that office that groups of women and schoolgirls had tried to stage sit-ins in support of the prisoner hunger strike then in its eleventh day when I left for the States in mid-October 1991. Many of the women had been mothers, grandmothers, or aunts of the prisoners and themselves had been fasting. I was standing outside the office when soldiers routed the gathering *shabab*, tore down banners, ripped up paper flags, and herded the women inside.

When Nidal called me on the evening of the anniversary commemoration, he was pleased. The day's program of poetry reading, speeches, chanting of slogans, and singing of national songs had been overseen by several international officers from the United Nations' refugee affairs program. Nidal was especially happy about the curfew. It had been the first in months under Prime Minister Rabin's hands-off policy on the West Bank: "You see, Janet," he said to me over the phone, "the army is still afraid of Mohammad Abu Aker after all this time."

More than once, I have wondered if money would have mattered so much in Mohammad Abu Aker's case had the Deaconess Hospital patient been a political refugee from Cuba or the former Eastern Bloc suffering the intestinal deterioration of Crohn's disease rather than a bullet-injured Intifada victim from a West Bank refugee camp. Mohammad's case may simply have become too hot a political potato, especially for a Christian hospital's board of directors, which, during the first two years of the Intifada, was more than likely sensitive to possible charges of anti-Semitism in extending free care to one of the uprising's young activists.

I have also wondered how PLO politics may have entered Mohammad's case, not so much on the West Bank as between its Tunis and Damascus headquarters. Fatah, which has its international offices in Tunis, was involved by way of Roots and the Naim Foundation in paying the first installment on Mohammad's bill and then refused to pay more; the Popular Front office in Damascus was to have overseen the second payment, which never came through—at least not all the way to the accounts receivable department at Deaconess Hospital. Did Mohammad's case vaporize, I have occasionally speculated, in the ideological distance that separates Yasser Arafat's Tunis and Dr. George Habash's Damascus, headquarters of the Popular Front?[10] Or was the explanation for the intractable money problem to be found in less murky and less dramatic circumstances? Perhaps Mohammad was simply a casualty of the overwhelmed good intentions of disorganized Arab-Americans trying somehow to meet the skyrocketing needs created by the uprising. Whatever the case, it is safe to say that his death was finally the result of multiple causes beyond the medical. Those causes may never be fully sorted out.

At news of Mohammad's death in October 1990, the Boston *shabab*, both Fatah and Popular Front supporters, met together in a Cambridge

church to commemorate the time they had had with the Deheishe teenager. Mandaris was the one who organized the memorial meeting. On the
second of Mohammad's visits, he had taken him to the Boston aquarium.
Mandaris had hoped to take Mohammad to the circus before his young
friend and idol had had to cut that last visit short.

Mandaris was born in a Palestinian refugee camp in Lebanon where
his parents had settled after the first Arab-Israeli war. For him as for mil-
lions like him in the diasporas of 1948 and 1967, the homeland had remained a construct of his political imagination. The "living martyr" must
have been a reminder of Palestine's distance from his own life even as
Mohammad's presence in Boston brought it momentarily closer. Some of
the wrangling among these groups of young men and women must have
been an uneasy response to the bittersweetness of that double fact.

Chapter 2

The Deheishe Story

The Israeli writer David Grossman made his first visit to Deheishe Camp in the early spring of 1986. In *The Yellow Wind*, Grossman describes what he saw in the "turbid rain" of that March afternoon. Beginning with the "ugly cement growths," as he calls the houses for the camp's multiplying population, Grossman goes on to describe Deheishe's open sewers and its children's runny noses as well as scanty grocery shelves and pitiful coffee-can gardens. On the first of two separate days he spent in the camp, Grossman went to the cramped hovel of Hadija, a very old woman, who, suspicious of the Israeli visitor, refused to talk with him. In the end, she shouted at him about the impossibility of his understanding her situation: "Culture! You people don't know that we have a culture! You can't understand this culture."[1]

I made my first visit to Deheishe some two and a half years later on a sunny morning in September 1988, ten months after the outbreak of the Intifada. Starting out from Jerusalem's Mount of Olives, where I had been visiting Mohammad at Makassad Hospital, I came to the camp in the company of Mohammad's father. We came by taxi and were dropped off beside the wall of the Abu Aker courtyard on the southern edge of the camp near a stone factory. What first met my eyes as I entered the courtyard gate was a garden full of roses, geraniums, daisies, phlox, and an ivy-like succulent that grew along the low wall between the garden and the tiled walkway and up the side of a substantial two-story house faced with pale pink stone. Bright blue morning glories entwined the railing of the stairs that led to the small balcony porch posted at either end with tall globed lamps and on the far side ending beside a large front door.

The house had been built on top of the cement-block structure in which Mohammad's mother had grown up and where her six children had been born. Part of the old structure now served as a laundry room, and the largest area, earlier the family's salon, had been turned into a large meeting room where six months later camp residents would be celebrating Mohammad's homecoming from the hospital. Two years later, the former salon would be filled with mourners at Mohammad's death. On the first anniversary of Mohammad's death, the downstairs would be in the early stages of transformation as future living quarters for Mohammad's brother Rafat and his wife-to-be.

The upper part of the house was finished in 1986, the year of David Grossman's visit to the camp. Built with family savings and the contributed labor of relatives, friends, and neighbors, the house opened through a double door into a traditional salon whose walls were lined with low cushions used during the day for sitting and at night for sleeping. To the right was a Western-style living room furnished with a long couch, a love seat, and four chairs, all of them upholstered in a plush gray fabric and arranged around a large glass and chrome coffee table. Four matching side tables were ready for the tea, coffee, and fruit juices served to the neighbors and young comrades who regularly congregated in the Abu Aker household as well as to the journalists and fact-finding groups who would be a regular part of the family's weekly and often daily routine for the remaining two years of Mohammad's second life.

Behind the two front rooms were a modern kitchen and bath. Three bedrooms were located off a long hallway that led to a large glassed-in veranda at the back of the house. Offering a panoramic view that went all the way down a steep hill to the Hebron-Jerusalem road, the veranda, I would come to know, was the most important room in the house. From the veranda the family and their friends would watch for the Israeli soldiers who patrolled the camp around the clock. To know exactly where they were in the camp was part of the day's, and sometimes the night's, regular agenda.

Mohammad's mother was the family's self-appointed sentinel. She was born Malka, but she was now known as Um Nidal, the mother of Nidal, having taken the name of her firstborn son, Rafat's twin brother, in accordance with Arab custom. Likewise, her husband, Naim, was known as Abu (father of) Nidal after the twins came along. From time to time over the subsequent years, I would be referred to as Um Adam, the mother of my son, Adam.

The first thing upon waking up and the last thing before going to bed, Malka would watch from the veranda. She was always the first person to spot a patrol rounding a corner, walking through a narrow pathway, assembling in front of a house, or stationing itself on a rooftop. At night, she would be the one to hear the sound of the soldiers' boots or see the point of light in the distance that identified a soldier lighting his cigarette. As I came to be a regular visitor over the next two years, I would watch along with her.

It was also in the veranda that Nidal and I would have our late-night talks about Deheishe's history of resistance and Nidal's hopes and dreams about his own future. One summer night when Nidal was talking with his friends about "the Situation," one of them, Ziad, suddenly turned to me and asked what my son and his friends would be doing. When I began to say something in general terms about their being in college, Ziad interrupted me, "Right now, I mean." Ignoring the time difference, I said Adam and his friends would most likely be talking about girls. "With a passion almost as intense as your own," I said, "when you talk about the Intifada." It was in this same veranda that Malka would say to me, "You have been running until you reached Deheishe."

Malka greeted me that September morning at the door off the balcony. Other members of the family were waiting to greet me as I walked into the traditional salon: Hazem, Mohammad's fourteen-year-old brother; Nida' and Hala, his ten- and six-year-old sisters; and his grandmother, whose exact age was unknown, but who was probably in her late eighties. Having made the pilgrimage to Mecca in her younger years (the *haj*, as it is called in Arabic), she was referred to as the *hajeh*, a term of respect for a woman who has made that holy journey.

Neither of the twins was there to welcome me. Rafat had been staying overnight at Makassad Hospital with Mohammad, whose drying skin he would no doubt be rubbing with Nivea cream, since Mohammad continued to lose large amounts of fluid through duodenal and rectal drainage. Nidal was about to finish three months of administrative detention in Ansar III, the large tent prison that had been set up (in violation of international law) in Israel's Negev Desert during the first year of the Intifada to accommodate a rapidly increasing population of Palestinian political prisoners like himself.[2] He had been in detention when Mohammad was shot, and the family was praying that he would be released in time to see his brother still alive.

Mohammad's great uncle, brother of the *hajeh*, was also on hand to greet me. Dapper in a suit and tie topped off by a traditional white head-dress and black band (*'igal*), the sixty-seven-year-old uncle had served in the British Mandate's Arab police force in the late thirties and early for-ties. I would be hearing many of his stories about the old days, often to the chagrin of the *shabab* (young male activists), who would raise their eye-brows when one of his stories went on too long. They were eager to ex-change news about current skirmishes, not to dwell on events from the past.

"Everything happens elsewhere," David Grossman had written. "Not now. In another place. In a splendid past or a longed-for future." In *The Yellow Wind*, the Israeli writer sees the uncle's seeming nostalgia about the old days everywhere. The Palestinians' "one real asset," Grossman claimed, is their "ability to wait." But even this dapper gentleman with British manners was no passive waiter: the uncle had been sentenced to four years in prison for possession of an antitank weapon, and while he was serving that sentence his house in Doha, across the road from De-heishe, was demolished in 1969 as collective punishment for his resis-tance activity.

Once again, I found a different Deheishe from the one Grossman de-scribed. The camp I came to know had a history not of patience but of making things happen. Deheishe was, for example, one of the first camps in the Occupied Territories to have a national unity movement. Although its resistance activity had been going on randomly even before 1967, first against the Jordanian monarchy and then against the Israeli Occupation, the camp's systematic organizing began around the time of Israel's inva-sion of Lebanon in 1982. Organizing involved the camp's young women as well as the young men, both groups forming clubs that in the early eighties undertook camp improvements like the resurfacing of main roads and distributing supplemental food and clothing to the camp's poorest residents. From 1985 on, these groups worked hard to maintain a unified front against collaborators' attempts to create rifts among the political parties they supported, mainly Dr. George Habash's Popular Front for the Liberation of Palestine and Yasser Arafat's Fatah. In smaller numbers, Deheishe residents also supported the Democratic Front, the Palestine Communist Party, and—in smaller numbers yet—Hamas, the Islamic resistance party newly formed during the Intifada.

The twenty-foot-high fence told much of Deheishe's more recent story. As indicated by the lengthening and increasingly reinforced fence, Deheishe's activism won the attention of Moshe Arens, then Israel's defense minister, who ordered the first phase of fence building in 1985, after residents clashed with Muslim Brotherhood members who infiltrated the camp in order to sow dissent. It is widely believed that at that time the Egypt-based Islamic group was supported by Israel as well as the CIA. Along with the fence, two army installations were set up close to the camp with twenty-four-hour patrolling that from then on became a regular part of Deheishe's day-to-day life.

The fence was extended in 1987 after a clash between residents and a group of about twenty invading settlers who went on a shooting rampage around midnight on June 6. Members of Gush Emunim (the Faithful Ones), a West Bank settlement movement that began shortly after the 1973 war, raided houses, shot at rooftop water tanks and solar panels, damaged cars, and torched one that was parked at a gas station across the road from the stone factory. In response to the settlers' rampage, the army clamped a three-day curfew on the camp and ordered all its males between sixteen and thirty-five to report to Bethlehem military headquarters for questioning. In addition to arresting seventeen youths, the military authorities permanently blocked off two main entrances to the camp and extended the partial fence the full length of the camp. They took this action to appease the settlers from Kiryat Arba, headquarters of the Gush Emunim movement in Hebron, who had long complained about the stoning of their cars on their way to and from Jerusalem.

The Intifada began six months after the rampage, and the wider Palestinian population quickly caught up with what Deheishe residents had been doing for decades. During the Intifada, corrugated zinc panels were added to the road side of the fence, and barbed wire was rolled out along its inside base. A turnstile replaced the main gate and smaller entrances were sealed off with metal barrels filled with concrete. But even almost-total enclosure failed to keep Deheishe from making things happen—not "in a splendid past or a longed-for future" or only in regular stoning of passing settler cars, but in acts of mundane resistance in the daily round, mostly by women like Malka who insisted on living their ordinary lives, visit by supportive visit (even under curfews) and cross-stitch by steadfast cross-stitch (even during home invasions).

Not until my return visit to the camp after the Gulf War did I hear the story of the founding of Deheishe. The story came from the father of

Ziad, one of the regular veranda *shabab*, by that time a student at Bethlehem University, where he was majoring in English. A man in his mid-sixties, Abu Ziad had spent a year in a tent prison, a smaller version of present-day Ansar III, for having protested against the new Jordanian monarchy under King Hussein in 1957. In 1974, seven years after the West Bank came under Israeli occupation, Abu Ziad spent ten days in jail for owning a book on the history of Palestine. A retired schoolteacher, he spent his time reading when he was not working in his garden.

Dressed always in a long and carefully pressed gray robe, a *dishdasheh*, Abu Ziad was a dignified man who loved the intricacies of the Arabic language he taught for thirty-seven years. Although he was reserved, he was the Deheishe resident often called on to preside over important public events like the opening of the camp's dental clinic in 1989. He had a reputation not only among the camp's elders but also with its youth for his sense of humor and storytelling ability.

I call him Abu Ziad, although Ziad was the third among his four sons. The oldest of Ziad's brothers was a civil engineer in Jordan whose work took him to many other parts of the Arab world. The second son earned a Ph.D. in chemistry in the former Soviet Union. The fourth son studied physics at Bethlehem University.

Education was clearly a priority in Abu Ziad's family, for the daughters as well as the sons. One of Ziad's two sisters has a master's degree in social work from a Chicago university. She was among the first women admitted to Bethlehem University in 1974. Her father encouraged her to enroll despite neighbors' cautions about studying with boys. She now teaches in a Ramallah nursing college. The other daughter, the first of the family's six children, was a staff nurse at Bethlehem's Mount David Orthopedic Hospital before she died of cancer at age forty-two.

Seated in the salon overlooking his beautifully landscaped garden, Abu Ziad began the story of Deheishe with his own flight from Zakariya, which, before the establishment of the state of Israel in 1948, was a Palestinian village at the southeast entrance to the Jerusalem corridor. In the months of fighting between 1947 and the beginning of 1948, Abu Ziad had been part of an uncertain and shifting Palestinian population that was afraid to stay in its villages but, at the same time, afraid to leave for what would turn out to be exile. Zakariya held out the longest against Zionist forces, according to the Israeli historian Benny Morris.[3]

Abu Ziad and his wife had been part of the last remnant who left following the Jews' murder of three Zakariya men just outside the village. A woman who witnessed the killing was allowed to return to the village to broadcast the news, which, along with the Deir Yassin massacre that had taken place five months earlier, had terrified the remaining villagers.[4] Except for the old and the sick, who were transported in several trucks, the rest of the villagers walked through the mountains to Hebron. "Our walk took fifteen days," Abu Ziad told me and then interrupted his narrative for a comment: "When you believe that the lives of your children are in danger, you leave your home. Look at the Kurds. You must have seen them on television." He was referring to the post-Gulf War coverage of the miserable plight of Kurdish refugees seen on television screens around the world. There had been no television coverage of that exile some forty-three years earlier. Even after all these years, Abu Ziad continued to feel shame at having left his land, despite the fact that it had not been by choice.

Thousands of villagers from the surrounding area, along with those from Zakariya, converged on Hebron. "We were lucky," Abu Ziad said. He and his wife along with members of his extended family, eight in all, were able to share a room for three months in a house belonging to a friend of his grandfather before going to a camp in Jericho where they joined a group of five thousand other exiles. Other camps, he said, housed up to forty thousand. They lived for another six months on meager food distributions from the Jordanian government, which refused them permission to plant the seeds they had managed to bring with them from Zakariya.

In June 1949, Abu Ziad's family and other former villagers from Zakariya moved to Deheishe, where most of them were to live in tents for seven years until the United Nations established a special branch, United Nations Relief and Works Agency (UNRWA), to administer Palestinian affairs and build cement-block houses for the "refugees," as Palestinian exiles like Abu Ziad and his family came to be called. The tent camp was at first administered by the International Committee of the Red Cross. Abu Ziad was elected his village's representative for food distribution since he could read and write and, as he said, "make lists." He was among the camp's thirty-six representatives from former Palestinian villages in the Jerusalem and Bethlehem districts, many of them among the more than four hundred villages, like Kufr Bir'im in the Upper Galilee, that were destroyed to make way for the new state of Israel.

Later in the year, Abu Ziad volunteered to begin a school, having been a teacher at the boys' school in Zakariya established in the late 1800s. He and four other volunteer teachers soon ran out of their own money for supplies and, with instructions from a cook from Jerusalem, they made banners to stage a protest, Abu Ziad told me. "Our banners read, 'We want chalk,' 'We want books,' and, on the largest banner of all, 'WE WANT TO GO HOME.' " With two hundred students who joined the protest, the five teachers walked to the Red Cross office in Bethlehem, shouting their demands along the way. Jordanian policemen on horseback took the banners and arrested the teachers. "I used my last fifty piasters to hire a car to take my colleagues and me to the Jerusalem court," he said. "The policemen managed to squeeze in with us."

The Jordanian government, which would administer the West Bank until it was defeated by Israel in the June war of 1967, acquitted the teachers but warned them against further protest. The teachers began a sit-in at the Bethlehem police station the next day. After four days, a local Red Cross representative called Geneva for instructions. "From then on," Abu Ziad said, "we received free supplies of books and chalk, and we teachers were paid."

Abu Ziad's tent was conveniently located near the school, but because it was pitched on low ground it got flooded during the winter rainy season. In the spring of 1950, Abu Ziad moved with his wife and baby daughter to higher ground on the far side of the camp. There were rocks, but no trees or vegetation. He started landscaping the area even before he began, room by room, building his house. "Mine was the first house in the camp," he said with some pride. Six years later, UNRWA started building more permanent structures for other Deheishe residents.

Abu Ziad then showed me around the garden he had established among the rocks in his courtyard. Every inch of soil was planted with flowers, shrubs, and fruit trees. "They knew almost every stone and every tree," the Palestinian writer Ghassan Kanafani had written about fellow exiles some five years after *Al-Nakba* (the Catastrophe of 1948). "Not only that," Kanafani wrote, "but they knew the history of each tree, who had owned it and who had acquired it, and how much it bore or did not bear, what would happen to it this season and what had happened to it last season."[5] Unable to return to his village, Abu Ziad has nonetheless been able to reproduce in miniature—and to tend the reproduction with as much intimate knowledge as—the orchard he had to leave behind in Zakariya.

Deheishe Camp currently houses 1,650 families on about four hundred acres of land. A population of about eight thousand, more than half under the age of sixteen, is served by a number of UNRWA programs including a physical therapy unit recently donated by Japan and a dental clinic funded primarily by individual contributions, including donations from camp families.

Employing 150 camp residents, UNRWA provides the primary source of income for camp residents. Another eighty-five work in nearby factories producing plastic products, cement, cigarettes, furniture, and building stones. A pool of about 350 day laborers who once made a living as construction workers or gardeners in Israel has increasingly been replaced by Soviet immigrants. Other families support themselves through small camp businesses: forty-five grocery rooms in UNRWA-built modules; fifteen house shops where several family members machine stitch garments out of precut pieces supplied by Israeli factories through Palestinian intermediaries; four olive wood "factories"; four garages for car repair; and two cavelike bakeries. Residents include two doctors, two lawyers, two pharmacists, three engineers, and eight journalists. There is a contingent of staff nurses who work in Bethlehem hospitals or at Jerusalem's Makassad and Augusta-Victoria Hospitals, the latter operating under the supervision of the Lutheran World Federation and serving the Palestinian refugee population on the West Bank.

Besides staff nurses, there is a growing number of practical nurses living in the camp. The ranks of the practical nurses are being filled mostly by young women recently graduated from high school who, unlike many of the young men, have identity cards allowing travel to Jerusalem or Ramallah for study. Because the young women's travel is so far unrestricted, they are becoming their family's chief, sometimes only, means of support, a fact that contributes to changes in their social and political status in the camp.

While the young women carry red cards, a high percentage of their male cohorts were issued restrictive green cards after being released from administrative detention or prison—simply for being regarded as security risks on the basis of their age and Deheishe residency. Green-card carriers are subject to being roughed up by army patrols and are forbidden to travel outside the West Bank, a restriction that puts off-limits most Palestinian educational programs (vocational or university) on the West Bank other than those at Bethlehem University, where although admission is limited by size and cost, travel connections in East Jerusalem (Israel-annexed territory out of bounds for Deheishe green-card holders) are made unnecessary.

"When all of Palestine becomes Deheishe," a camp resident told me before I left for the United States in the summer of 1990, "we will get our state." What he said reminded me of what Ghassan Kanafani, the camp's patron saint, called the "true Palestine." Neither a territory nor a dogma, his "true Palestine" was a process more than a piece of geography, an ongoing life of struggle to be found more often among inarticulate villagers and camp residents than among urban intellectuals like himself. Kanafani had grown up in a refugee camp in Damascus after he and his family were forced to leave the Palestinian port city of Acre in 1947. Before he was assassinated by a Mossad car bomb in 1972, Kanafani contributed several novels and dozens of short stories to the body of resistance literature his writing helped to define.[6]

In a letter to his young son, Fayiz, Kanafani describes the process of loss and recovery that accompanied Fayiz's sudden recognition of himself as a Palestinian. Kanafani had overheard his son asking his mother, "Mama, am I a Palestinian?" When the boy's question was answered in the affirmative, "a heavy silence fell on the whole house," Kanafani said. "It was as if something hanging over our head had fallen, its noise exploding, then—silence." Hearing his son crying in the next room, "it was as if a blessed scalpel was cutting up your chest and putting there the heart that belongs to you," the father wrote. Through the boy's "bewildered tears," the father imagined "that a distant homeland was being born again: hills, plains, olive groves, dead people, torn banners and folded ones, all cutting their way into a future of flesh and blood and being born in the heart of another child."[7] The "true Palestine" was being born in Fayiz—in effect, it was a transplanted heart whose embodiment of the homeland depended, first of all, on the fully realized experience of its loss. The "true Palestine" was being born out of both sadness and hope, ongoing struggle and steadfastness.[8]

Another Kanafani letter, this one fiction, depicts a similar alteration in perception, a kind of conversion experience combining memory of loss and hope of recovery. Featuring an unnamed Gazan schoolteacher who, like Kanafani himself, taught Palestinian refugee children in an UNRWA school, "Letter from Gaza" operates through a series of reversals and inversions by which the ugly is transformed into purposefulness, vulnerability converts to power, the site of loss becomes the ground for reclamation, and fantasies about California are supplanted by Gaza reality.

Compressed in a story that takes up only four pages and even further concentrated into less than an hour of the protagonist's experience, the rapid-fire series of inversions is framed by two surprise announcements, one at the beginning of the letter and one at the end, that overturn the lifelong intention of the letter writer and his friend Mustafa to exchange Gaza's "ugly debris of defeat" for the promising life awaiting them in the West. The schoolteacher had finally saved enough from a year's teaching in Kuwait to be able to join Mustafa, who had left for America some years earlier and had finally arranged for his friend to study civil engineering at the University of California while sharing living quarters in Sacramento. At the end of his first paragraph, however, the letter writer announces an abrupt change of plans:

> No, my friend, I have changed my mind. I won't follow you to 'the land where there is greenery, water, and lovely faces' as you wrote. No, I'll stay here, and I won't ever leave.[9]

The remainder of the letter is given over to describing the circumstances that brought the letter writer to the decision that so suddenly changed the course of both lives. His letter ends with yet another surprising reversal. Not only has he decided against following his friend to America; he now asks that Mustafa return to Gaza: "Come back, my friend! We are all waiting for you." As we soon learn, the most fundamental reversal involves the transformed perspective that comes with the schoolteacher's discovery about himself: like Kanafani's son, he suddenly and painfully realizes that he is a Palestinian.

On returning from Kuwait with the money he had put aside for his escape to the West, the letter writer had planned to stay in Gaza just long enough to pack his bags for California. The place seemed all the more ugly—much like the ugliness David Grossman saw in Deheishe that dreary March afternoon—in contrast to the beauty he imagines awaiting him in America. The "narrow streets" of the Shajiya quarter, where the letter writer and his friend grew up, smells of "defeat and poverty"; the neighborhood houses disgust him "with their bulging balconies":

> I found Gaza just as I had known it, closed like the introverted lining of a rusted snail-shell thrown up by the waves on the sticky, sandy shore by the slaughterhouse. This Gaza was more cramped than the mind of a sleeper in the throes of a fearful nightmare. (88)

For the Gazan just returning from Kuwait and on his way to California, "everything in the amputated town reminded [him] of failed pictures painted in grey by a sick man" (87).

The word *amputated* prepares the reader for Kanafani's *scalpel* and the debridement and transplant needed to make way for converting loss into recovery, defeat into victory, the lifeless wasteland into a throbbing homeland. Kanafani's protagonist comes under the scalpel when, at the persuasion of his widowed sister-in-law, he agrees to visit his thirteen-year-old niece in the hospital before setting off for his new life in America. Nadia had been injured in an Israeli raid that took place in the middle of her uncle's school year in Kuwait.[10]

Admitting to Mustafa how little difference the raid made to him at the time, the letter writer is about to experience an "explosion" all the more forceful for its delay, "as if something hanging over our head had fallen," Kanafani had written to his son, "its noise exploding." Soon after entering the hospital room, the letter writer discovers that Nadia's leg had been amputated "from the top of her thigh." In the violent rebirthing that follows, the streets of Gaza had "filled . . . with the colour of blood" when the letter writer walks out of the hospital; with a radically transformed understanding about himself, he sees his old town, too, as newly born. The epiphany continues:

> Gaza was brand new, Mustafa! You and I never saw it like this. The stones piled up at the beginning of the Shajiya quarter where we lived had a meaning, and they seemed to have been put there for no other reason than to explain it. This Gaza in which we had lived and with whose good people we had spent seven years of defeat [since the Catastrophe of 1948] was something new. (89)

Nadia's disabling "wound" enabled her uncle to recognize what it means to be a "true" Palestinian. As he says to Mustafa at the outset, "I have never seen things so clearly as I do now." Not simply the product of intellectual enlightenment, the uncle's new way of seeing and feeling is as immediate as the beating of his own heart:

> Everything in this [new] Gaza throbbed with sadness which was not confined to weeping. It was a challenge; more than that, it was something like reclamation of the amputated leg!

His conversion of perspective embodies itself as the experience of a phantom limb, a presence making itself all the more known in its very absence.

"Do not believe that man grows," Kanafani wrote at the end of the letter to his son. "No; he is born suddenly—a word, in a moment, penetrates his heart to a new throb. One scene can hurl him down from the ceiling of childhood on to the ruggedness of the road" (2). The experience that had cut its way into the hearts of the two letter writers, Kanafani and his unnamed Gazan, generated in both a lifelong practice of *sumud* (steadfastness).

The story of Deheishe continues for me with the current lives of Nasser and his older brother, the former living in the camp's family compound with his wife and young twins, the latter living in a New Jersey apartment with his American wife. I met Nasser several days after the death of Mohammad Abu Aker in October 1990 and less than a month after Nasser had been released from prison. Along with three other young men from the camp, he had served a five-year sentence for a 1985 attack on a Palestinian collaborator, a policeman in the employ of the West Bank Israeli civil administration who had threatened Deheishe residents with an ax. From the beginning of the uprising, most of the Palestinian police force resigned under pressure from the Intifada leadership. Many policemen publicly repented in mosques during the first year of the uprising and were accepted back into their communities.

An eighteen-year-old sophomore when soldiers took him off a bus carrying Bethlehem University students to a day's outing in Jaffa, Nasser had just returned to classes again when I met him among the steady flow of mourners coming to pay their respects to the Abu Akers. We spent most of that first meeting talking about a recent visit from his brother, who was then just finishing his Ph.D. in the States.

Nasser's brother Hisham had begun his graduate program in the fall of 1985, just a month after Nasser was arrested. Nasser's sentence had not yet been announced when the older brother left the West Bank for the United States. The family was preparing itself for a possible twenty years, which Nasser knew would be harder on his brother than on him. "Hisham has an academic mind," Nasser explained; "he has difficulty understanding these things." As it turned out, the younger brother would be getting a Palestinian-style education at Hebron Prison while the older brother was spending the same five years at a prestigious New England university. When I eventually met Hisham, he would tell me that Nasser viewed his years in prison as a loss of ten years when their respective five-year periods of separation were combined.

Nasser knows that Deheishe values his status as a former prisoner as highly as his brother's doctorate, maybe more, but he also knows that the rest of the world sees their respective situations in very different terms. He knows, too, about the temptation to join the thinking of the rest of the world, especially when he is in his university classes in sociology and psychology. "I must sometimes hurry back to Deheishe," he told me, "to keep things straight in my own mind."

Nasser told me two stories that illustrate the differences now between himself and Hisham. During the latter's visit, a three-day curfew was imposed on the camp after a stone-throwing demonstration. While Hisham was annoyed at the curfew, Nasser was interested only in whether it was Popular Front or Fatah supporters who threw the stones. Another stone-throwing incident took place in the camp a week later while Nasser was at military headquarters in Bethlehem to apply for the permanent identity card that would replace the temporary paper issued to him when he was released from prison. When he returned to Deheishe shortly after the demonstrating youths had dispersed, he and a friend were picked up as suspected stone throwers and taken back to military headquarters. Only because Nasser was able to waylay a passing clerk who vouched for the fact that Nasser had been at the headquarters at the time of the demonstration was he saved from the imprisonment and stiff fine that likely awaited the young man who was picked up with him.

Hisham was enraged by the arbitrariness of life under occupation. "Why wouldn't your friend take his case to court?" he had asked. "After five years away," Nasser said, "my brother has forgotten about the way things are with us." It is a rare case that is won by Palestinians in courts administered by the Israeli military government. More often than not, the courts are places of humiliation where rules of evidence do not exist.

Nasser recalled their initial silence as they sat, just the two of them, in the salon. "We were unable at first to speak to one another," he said to me; "I wanted so badly for Hisham to tell me about America, but he refused to talk about his own five years. Instead, he kept asking me about my experience in prison and about the situation in the camp." I asked Nasser if he knew Kanafani's "Letter from Gaza." When he said he had read it in high school, I suggested he might read it again. I was thinking of the confusion Mustafa must have experienced when his friend not only refused to join him in America but also urged him to return to Gaza.

Nasser's brother remembers other things about the visit, as I learned over a weekend I spent with him and his wife in their New Jersey apartment some sixteen months later. Kim's blond hair was in a ponytail, so she looked much younger than she did in the photographs that Nasser had shown me. And only when I met him face to face was I struck by the close resemblance between Hisham and his mother, who is just as petite as Kim.

Hisham was just finishing a postdoctoral year at a telecommunications headquarters in Princeton when I finally met him nearly a year and a half after meeting Nasser. Since the academic job market was tight, he was hoping to be kept on at the company. He and Kim mentioned the Jeep Cherokee they would buy if a regular job contract came through. Kim, in the last stages of writing her dissertation, was scheduling job interviews at several area colleges where she could teach chemistry. "My job applications are having better luck than my husband's," she told me. The couple had met at the university, where he had been her lab instructor. They had been married the previous fall, around the time I returned once again to Deheishe for the anniversary of Mohammad Abu Aker's death. The family did not attend the wedding. Nasser had been refused a laissez-passer to leave Israel. "My mother and father speak no English," Nasser had said to me, "so they would have been nervous to travel so far without me along."

The couple's one-bedroom apartment was part of a large development. Noting how different things were from "back home," Hisham told me they had not yet talked with any of their neighbors, a situation unimaginable in Deheishe, where neighbors were often in hourly communication with one another. Another difference hit him every time he arrived at his front door. Rosenfeld was the name on the nameplate just above his. "Arabs and Jews lived next to one another in Palestine," he said, "but that was a long time ago."

I was impressed by how settled their apartment seemed. It gave little sign of their being newlyweds or that their student days were not far behind. I was also struck by how insistently American it looked, with its intimate arrangement of living-room furniture rather than couches and chairs that hugged the walls as they did in Deheishe's Western-style salons. Their kitchen was fully equipped with a food processor and matched cooking utensils above the stove, the bathroom color coordinated with towels that matched the shower curtain.

That their place looked so defined was the result of what was absent as much as of what was there. Other than several photographs and a cross-stitched couch pillow in a traditional Palestinian design, I found nothing Middle Eastern in their surroundings. With a trace of sadness in his voice, Nasser's brother admitted that he spoke little Arabic anymore and, except for the hummus and dried seeds the couple buys occasionally from a Palestinian grocery in Newark, Hisham eats mostly American dishes. I joked with him about his becoming not only Americanized but also de-Palestinianized when I discovered that he permits Kim's two cats to sleep with them. But I, too, felt sad about how much he seemed to be giving up for a life on the other side of the world from Deheishe.

What Hisham told me about the reunion with Nasser began with his memory of their feeling lost together in the new political setting. Things had changed for both of them as a result of a revolution from which they had both been absent. Neither, up until that month, had experienced the Intifada, which had begun some two years after they had gone their respective ways to prison in Hebron and to a university in the United States.

The older brother recalled how he had accompanied Nasser to the Bethlehem office so that Nasser could exchange the temporary paper for his predictably green identity card. New regulations had been introduced into Occupation procedures; new words like *bingo*, Palestinian slang for being on the wanted list, had entered the lexicon; new shortcuts had been established to get around increased military checkpoints. Their trip to the Bethlehem office, the brother told me, "was a case of the blind leading the blind," since both of them had been out of circulation for so long. What struck him most was how much they needed to rely on one another.

Moving backward in the actual order of events, Nasser's brother then told me about his first night back in the camp. Instead of remembering the awkward silence in the salon, he recalled how lots of people arrived earlier in the day to greet both him and Nasser. As the day stretched into evening, Hisham admitted his tiredness and his impatience for the well-wishers to leave. At the same time, he felt himself to be an outsider and was nervous about being alone with the family, especially with Nasser. Once the visitors had left, his sister talked for a long time about what both brothers had missed during the past five years. Together they were catching up with and facing all the changes over the time each had been separated from Palestinian society. The visitors and his sister's report eased his reentry, Hisham confessed to me. They helped delay what he called his "plunge into the obscure"—an obscurity filled, as I imagined, by the guilt he felt for having left Deheishe.

In preparation for their sons' return to the camp, the parents used all the savings from the small grocery their father had run since the brothers were children to build a new kitchen and add four new rooms to their

UNRWA-built house. More than a welcome-home gift for the sons, the new surroundings were meant to communicate the parents' strong hope that their oldest son would return from America and that their younger son would be married as soon as possible to minimize the possibility of his being sent back to prison. The second of their wishes had been fulfilled: Nasser's wedding—a gala affair whose singing, dancing, and good food were a first in Deheishe Camp since the Intifada, when such occasions were discouraged—took place about ten months after his release from prison. Hisham, for whatever reason, had not attended.

He recalled with me how, after being led through the new family quarters in Deheishe, his father had turned to him: "I am waiting now for you to join us," he announced to his firstborn son. When I heard this, it occurred to me that the reason for the family's not coming to their oldest son's wedding in the States might lie beyond the refusal of Nasser's travel permit. For the parents to have come to the stateside wedding would have been for them to acknowledge the very real possibility that their oldest son will never again live in Palestine. Until they make that visit, New Jersey can perhaps continue to be nothing more than a strange postmark or a telephone connection. In the meantime, the father can hold on to the dream of having both his sons back under the family roof.

Nasser told me on our first meeting in the Abu Aker courtyard that he hoped to study philosophy, possibly in France, after completing his psychology degree at Bethlehem University: "Now that I am forced to see our life through my brother's eyes as well as my own, I can understand how important it is to develop a Palestinian philosophy which makes sense in the West." When Hisham left for the States again after their long-awaited reunion, he had asked Nasser to write him letters about day-to-day life, leaving out politics. Nasser had begun a first letter during the curfew imposed when two Deheishe youth, Lutfi and Iman, had been shot. "How can I keep politics out of my letters?" he asked me. Hisham later told me he wants to continue to support Nasser's schooling and hopes he will go on to earn a graduate degree in philosophy. "It will help me feel less guilty for leaving Deheishe," he said.

By the time I visited the New Jersey couple, they had received news of the twins born to Nasser's wife. A boy and a girl, they had been named Marcel and Beirut, the boy for the famous national singer Marcel Khalifeh, the girl for the one-time capital of Palestinian politics and culture before the PLO was forced out of Lebanon.

The couple were planning their first joint visit to Deheishe when I saw them. Kim's mother was nervous about her going, but Kim was calmly trying to learn as much Arabic as she could before leaving in the middle of the summer. She was excited about meeting the young nephews and nieces whose photographs were displayed in their apartment. Despite the fact that Hisham was settling into a life of cats and dreams of four-wheel-drive utility vehicles, he confessed to me that he could imagine nothing worse than losing his connection to Deheishe. "Nasser is the key to my connection," he said. "He's the one who keeps me in line, my 'moral watch.' "

"The average stay in this apartment complex is one year," Nasser's brother had told me. "People are passing through on their way to some-where else." He, too, seemed to be passing through. Despite the fact that his immediate surroundings revealed little about his past, it was nonethe-less clearer to me where he came from than where he was going. Late in our Saturday-night conversation, Kim by then asleep, Hisham made a fi-nal confession: "What I would really like to do someday is own a grocery store. I'm much more like my father than Nasser is." The older brother may not need to return to Deheishe. Clearly, he had brought it with him to New Jersey.

Chapter 3

"What Does It Mean Human?"

American Jewish novelist Bernard Malamud writes about Jews who survived the Holocaust. "What does it mean human?" asks a character in one of Malamud's many stories set on the lower East Side of New York City. Living in the New World, his Jewish characters nonetheless continue to wear their Old-World suffering like a suit of clothes: Breibert, the lightbulb peddler; Morris Bober, the struggling grocer; even Frank Alpine, Bober's Italian-American assistant, who, discovering from the grocer the meaning of his own suffering, gets circumcised and converts to Judaism.

The Holocaust is never far away from the day-to-day struggles of Malamud's grocers and peddlers in down-and-out American urban neighborhoods, barely two steps beyond the Eastern European shtetls from which they managed to escape. In the mundane lives of these characters, Malamud's stories embody in human-sized terms the ongoing legacy of a larger-than-life system of state-sponsored violence against the human.

When I ask what it means to be human, I have in mind the humanity the Palestinians, as well as Malamud's Jewish characters, keep a tight hold on while they live their ordinary lives under conditions that are designed to diminish, distort, and finally crush that humanity. Often stubborn, sometimes naive, occasionally foolish, Palestinian insistence on the daily is finally their strongest weapon against the Israeli Occupation. Over decades of struggle, and especially during the Intifada, that insistence has become both more pronounced and more tacit—pronounced, because its cost in life and limb has risen; tacit, because resistance goes increasingly without saying. The following stories about shopping for dates, delivering food to rabbits, and replenishing a supply of marbles as well as events relating to the assassination of birds and bees and the waging of war with laundry and children's kites are about Palestinian insistence on being human. Some call it *sumud*, or steadfastness.

In asking what it means to be human, I mean to ask as well about the human in human rights work. I am talking here about my own humanity. After all, the stories I tell were filtered through my humanness, the declared and undeclared baggage of past experiences as well as the "subject positions" I occupy—in their broadest strokes as white, Western, middle-aged, middle-class, and female. No disinterested account of the way things are, the parts I entitle "On losses, welcomes, and the all-too-human," "The high cost of living: other visits to Makassad," and "Celebrating survival" show how human rights work both engages and is engaged by lives of tenacity and hope in a West Bank refugee camp and a hospital full of Intifada casualties. Indeed, those other lives encouraged me, instructed me, and afforded me solace when I was ready to throw up my hands.

Like Malamud's stories, these Palestinian stories are about the mundane, and they, too, embody the larger technocratics of oppression. Part of what I call the Small News about the Intifada, they are stories about everyday life behind the bang-bang headlines, stories about how, in the midst of gross violations of their rights, Palestinians, like Malamud's Jewish characters, keep on. Though they are similar in human scale, the two sets of stories divide in the characters' responses to their respective situations: Malamud's characters wear their suffering as a badge of their humanity. When Frank Alpine becomes a Jew, he is, in effect, acknowledging his membership in a quintessentially human community: to be human is to suffer.[1]

The Palestinian stories deliver a different message: to be human is to resist. Although the stone has become its best-known instrument, Palestinian resistance also takes place at a less palpable level. Its truer emblem is to be found in the resolve to keep hold on the ordinary, no matter what. To comparison shop for dates in the middle of a clash, to deliver dried bread to rabbits under a curfew, to risk injury, even death, for the sake of continuing a game of marbles—these are instances of the resistance now built into Palestinian life in Gaza and the West Bank. More than living it, Palestinians insist on *leading* that life. Suffering it is not enough.

A Gazan woman shops for dates

We were seven passengers and the driver in the Mercedes taxi that is part of the Palestinian transportation system. The last to get into the taxi were a woman and her daughter who sat next to me in the middle row of seats. I sat as close to the window as I could scrunch to accommodate the daughter's bulk. In the back seat were a mother and her two grown sons. A well-dressed woman from Jerusalem sat in the front seat next to the driver.

Shortly after we got under way from Gaza City's Palestine Square, the taxi driver stopped at a small market just inside the city limits. The woman on my row of seats got out to price the dates that were lined up, large and shiny, in one of the stalls. She returned to the taxi without buying any. Just after we had passed under the "Welcome to Gaza" sign (in French and English), she motioned for the driver to take a detour to the adjacent village of Beit Hanoun. Ahead of us, as we approached the village center, soldiers were shooting tear gas canisters at a group of schoolgirls. To our side, women were lined up in front of the shops, screaming at helmeted soldiers as youths were running down an alley to escape their bullets. Clearly, we had driven into the middle of a clash.

It was just as clear that nothing would deter the mission on which we had set out: the woman on my bank of seats had to find dates at a better price. In the middle of the melee, she got out of the taxi, pinched the dates, and, having agreed to the asking price, carefully selected the half-kilo she decided to buy. At a still unhurried pace, she stepped into the taxi with a look of satisfaction on her face.

Then we just sat, waiting for the taxi driver to figure the best way to get out of the village. He finally switched on the ignition, turned the vehicle around, and slowly began to make his way back to the village entrance. On the way out, a villager tried to stop us so that we could take along an injured youth. The driver kept going, shouting "Al-Quds," the Arabic name of Jerusalem, out the window to indicate that he was on his way there and unwilling to turn around and go back to Gaza City. A United Nations ambulance was coming into the village as we neared the main road, where a parked army jeep looked as though it might block our exit. But the driver kept on going. Except for my roar of relief as we made the turn, we sailed down the highway as though there were nothing worth remarking.

Another half hour down the road, the date woman made unmistakable signs of needing to throw up. As she began to gag, I shouted to the taxi driver to stop and pull over. But all she demanded was a cigarette, whose smoke she inhaled deeply and held in her lungs to quell her nausea. When she rolled down her window to spit, her spittle flew into the back seat and hit the young man just behind me. He angrily wiped himself and tried to curl up fetal fashion in his corner.

The drive was further uneventful until ten minutes outside Jerusalem, when the defiled young man suddenly reached across his mother and slapped his brother on the face. A punching and shouting match started up between the two young men. As the altercation became more heated, both mothers began crying and the overweight daughter at my side became more and more agitated.

All of us passengers piled out of the taxi before it came to a full stop at the Jerusalem taxi stand across from Damascus Gate. I learned from the woman who had sat up front that the one mother was taking her daughter to a Bethlehem institution that treats behavioral disorders. Since soldiers beat her on the head three years ago, the daughter's behavior had become increasingly erratic. The other mother, it turned out, was taking her one son back to the hospital that a month before had treated him after his release from prison. Treatment under harsh interrogation and solitary confinement had left him, too, with increasingly severe behavioral disorders. I tried to recall what Nidal had once told me about the connection between dates and Mary, the mother of Jesus. Even if I had remembered, it would have brought little comfort to the mothers in the taxi.

A "mission of mercy" under curfew

"I want to deliver some dried bread to my brother's rabbits," Ghada said to me on a late-afternoon visit to the Abu Akers. "Why don't you come along?" she added. Ghada reminds me a lot of Mohammad's mother. She is high-spirited and just as undauntable as Malka, except, as it turned out, when it comes to mice. Even though the camp was under curfew and her brother lived on the other side of the camp, we decided to take our chances. Women and young children have better luck than men when they break a curfew. If we ran into a patrol, we would tell the soldiers that we were on a mission of mercy. Since Ghada had brought along her eight-month-old daughter, we could count on her protection as well as my American passport.

Our mission required a stop at Ghada's to pick up the bread. As far as her house, we could take a circuitous route through neighboring compounds, thereby avoiding the larger pathways that the army patrolled on their regular rounds in the camp. Naim decided to accompany us to that point.

We succeeded in avoiding any patrol on the way to Ghada's house. The box of bread was sitting in an outside shed. As Ghada was about to pick it up, a mouse poked its head above the discarded crusts. Ghada screamed and Naim quickly took the box outside the gate and put it down on the pathway in front of the compound. While Ghada stood at some distance, I took it upon myself to flush out the mouse. As soon as I stirred the contents of the box, the animal leaped out and scurried across the pathway.

Naim picked up a stone and was about to throw it at the mouse, Ghada squealing and me laughing, when a patrol of eight soldiers passed between Naim's raised hand and the mouse, whose escape was blocked by a wall on the other side of the path. Instead of detaining Naim and ordering Ghada and me back inside the compound, all the soldiers laughed except for the last one in line. He was too young to appreciate the set comic scene: a squealing woman, a cowering mouse, a heroic man who comes to the rescue. The seven soldiers continued to laugh as they turned a corner. By that time, the mouse had scampered off. The patrol had saved the mouse; the mouse had performed a miracle: for ten long seconds, we were all part of the same human community. Over tea at Ghada's we decided that completing our mission of mercy could wait until the curfew was lifted.

Anwar renews his marble supply

Round rubber bullets were introduced into the Israeli military arsenal in the first year of the Intifada for the announced purpose of crowd control. Cores of lead thinly covered with urethane, they proved lethal when shot at close range, eighteen at a time, from a specially fitted magazine on an automatic rifle. Eleven-year-old Anwar has facial scars from such bullets, but he, like other Deheishe boys, collects them for marble games.

One afternoon, Anwar scored badly in a marble game and lost his ready supply. The next thing anybody knew, he was standing on the roof of a house across the road from the military station. A soldier saw him and, as Anwar anticipated, aimed his rifle in Anwar's direction. Five minutes later, Anwar was back in the game with ten or so of the bullets that had landed on the roof, luckily avoiding any new scars for the time being.

Many people, including Palestinians themselves, have lamented the loss of childhood in the Intifada, when boys have to grow up too fast. No one, to my knowledge, has checked this out with Anwar, who insists on being a child even if it kills him. Foolish as well as dangerous, actions such as his, the date woman's, and Ghada's at the same time illustrate the steadfastness that has operated at the center of Palestinian consciousness for decades. "We must live our life," Palestinians keep saying, even though they risk losing it in the process.

A few counterpoint stories

When so many human beings have been imprisoned, beaten, and shot to death, the shooting of songbirds, the teargassing of bees, the burning of laundry, and the "war" on children's kites are hardly worth mentioning. But these seemingly incidental actions carried out by Israeli soldiers during the second year of the Intifada confirm both the deepening level of Palestinian resistance and the need to counter it. Resistance that goes all the way down must be met with attempts at the same register to destroy that very dailiness. The killing fields are saturated with the quotidian; the fundamental war is being waged at the level of the mundane.

As'ad, a Palestinian field-worker at the human rights center, told me about the songbird incident he had investigated in Khan Yunis, one of eight refugee camps in Gaza. "Soldiers raided our home in search of my brother," the field-worker's nineteen-year-old informant had said to As'ad. "When they didn't find him," the informant continued, "they beat my father and shot another of my brothers." The young man had reported his story with relative calm up to that point. "But he broke down," As'ad said, "when he told me how one of the soldiers turned around and shot his caged song sparrow on the way out of the house." As'ad, too, had tears in his eyes when he finished telling me the brief story.

The story about the teargassing of honeybees came from a West Bank field-worker who now lives with his wife and new son in a Jerusalem sub-urb north of Beit Hanina. The field-worker came from the village of Batir, where his father keeps bees. Their honey, which I had been privileged to taste, must have come from the same line of bees that, centuries ago, had supplied honey to the wandering Israelites. "It is heavenly," I told the field-worker.

Famous for its resistance, Batir became known as one of the "liber-ated" villages on the West Bank. It had undergone dozens of raids, sieges, and curfews during the Intifada. On a typical raid, soldiers would round up all the men between the ages of fourteen and sixty in the schoolyard, confiscate their identity cards, arrest a score of them, and get the rest to remove all the flags and graffiti that would readorn the village as soon as the army left and the youths could hoist more flags over the electric wires and get out their spray paint. On the most recent raid, the field-worker informed me, his father's bees had been teargassed. Like the shooting of the song sparrow, the gassing of the bees was more than an afterthought. Attempts at total dehumanizing had to include the destruction of what-ever might please the palate as well as the ear.

The laundry incident took place in Gaza's Jabaliya Camp, whose refu-gee population of 67,000 is the largest in the Occupied Territories. Jaba-liya had been my introduction to life under not-so-benign occupation when I visited the camp as part of the alternative tour I took in the winter of 1987. Appropriately enough, the laundry incident took place on a Monday—"Monday, wash day," as the song from my childhood had it. The story was reported the next day, July 18, 1989, in the *Jerusalem Post*. According to the *Post*, there had been "extensive unrest" in the camp on that Monday. Angered by the unrest, soldiers had "collected laundry of eight families, poured petrol on it and set it alight." By carefully ascribing the story to "Palestinian sources" and ending its ten-line report with a quote from an army spokesman who said that "no complaint of such an incident has been received," the newspaper unwittingly gave weight to the incident even as it treated it with mock seriousness. That it was only the cheap apparel of refugees the army attacked was, in fact, clear testi-mony to the lengths to which a bunch of pissed-off soldiers were pre-pared to go in quelling the uprising and venting their own frustration.

Even more telling was the "kites war" in Nablus. It, too, had been re-ported in the *Jerusalem Post*, just a few days before the laundry burning. The newspaper's own words need no further comment:

The kites war in Nablus continued yesterday as troops shot at two children's kites, bringing down only one, a Nablus resident told *The Jerusalem Post*.

Also in Nablus, soldiers confiscated the identity card of a resident of the town's Old City, forcing him to bring five kites from children in the neighborhood. Two months ago, according to the same source, the IDF [Israel Defence Force, which Palestinians prefer to call the Occupation Army] sent a helicopter to disperse balloons flying over Nablus. (July 10, 1989)

Such incidents reveal more than random lack of discipline, gratuitous cruelty, or simply boredom on the part of the military. In their very mundaneness, the killing of birds and bees, an attack on laundry, and a war on kites and balloons can best be understood as the appropriate response to a revolution that grounds itself in the most ordinary aspects of everyday life. Responding in kind, the soldiers seemed at some level to be aware of that fearful fact. Rejecting both nostalgia about the past and unrealistic dreams about the future, the Palestinian uprising is about living life *now*, about seizing today, not yesterday or tomorrow, for being fully human.

The human in human rights: On losses, welcomes, and the all-too-human

Journal Entry/October 14, 1989   From time to time, I inventory all the things I have lost in my life. I happened to remember another item to add to my list just before I came back from the States two weeks ago, Max Roach's *Freedom Now Suite*, a record album I bought in Philadelphia back in 1961 and must have lent to someone, maybe in Chicago, maybe in North Carolina. I know I couldn't find it when I was sorting out all the property I would be taking with me to Greensboro when my husband and I separated. I left him a note about it, but he was not able to find it among his part of the record collection we had divided.

Somehow I had forgotten this item until I was on a whirlwind cross-country tour speaking on what I called the "Small News of the Intifada." I jotted down "Freedom Now" on a slip of paper along with something else that I figured should be on the Lost List. I have since misplaced the piece of paper and have forgotten what the second item was.

Keeping my list accurate and up to date is important. It is usually in the middle of the night that I go over it. It dates all the way back to that kitchen spoon I never recovered from the hole I dug next to the Bozichs'. What fills the most recent part of my list are the items that have been stolen, first in Greensboro some months before I left for Jerusalem last year and then this past April when I moved from Shofat to the Sheikh Jarrah neighborhood of East Jerusalem. The first robbery happened over the Valentine's Day weekend in 1988 when I had flown to Chicago to talk over with a friend the decision I was then making to leave my job and return to the Middle East. I discovered when I returned that my Fisher Park house had been broken into and almost all of my gold jewelry taken: three gold chains, one of them belonging to my grandmother, and two rings—the engagement diamond I had had reset in a deco band that belonged to my grandfather ("Da-dat") and the cocktail ring I had had designed for my mother on her sixtieth birthday.

Who robbed me in Greensboro, I never found out. But there was no question about who stole the items in April, because the guilty party, a Palestinian who moved my furniture in his family's Mack truck, returned several of the things after I threatened to go to the police. Still missing, though, is an old Parker pen that belonged to my Great Aunt Mary, my grandmother's sister with the ill-fitting dentures.

There is also no question about why I keep my list going. A kitchen spoon, several pieces of jewelry, a pen, and Max Roach's album are clearly stand-ins for other losses I am unable to name or unwilling to keep so clearly in mind. I find it unsettling that I continue to keep such a hold on my list in a place where I am developing the capacity to feel at home.

Ahlen wasahlen: these are the Arabic words of greeting when you are welcomed into someone's house. Omar, my language teacher, explained the full meaning of the phrase a few weeks before I left for the States. His translation went something like this: *Ahlen wasahlen*, now that you have come into our home, you are another member of our family. The place you have entered is a level plain where the words we speak to one another will be clear and our feelings true and unobstructed. At the finish of his explanation, I cried out in astonishment that there could be such a place, but also in recognition of my having found it in the Abu Aker household at Deheishe Camp.

How foolish I was to have feared the loss of this welcome as a result of what had happened during the forty days I spent back in the United States. The nearly three weeks on the road from North Carolina and Kentucky to California and then back to Boston by way of Colorado, Iowa, and Wisconsin were filled with good things. My Deheishe readings went well, my reunions with old friends affirmed the decision I had made to return to the Middle East, and my manuscript was now in the hands of a large trade publisher.[2]

But all the while, things were going from bad to worse for Mohammad, who accompanied me as far as Boston, where I left him undergoing physical exams while I was off on my speaking tour. I had spent several months arranging for him to come with me, but he had had to return alone to the West Bank.

I got back to Jerusalem in the middle of a five-day general strike that kept Arab buses and taxis off the road. I was grateful for the reprieve the strike gave me because I was afraid of what I might find when I went to the camp to see Mohammad and his family. I felt sure that the Boston fiasco would have served only to underscore Mohammad's continuing dependence on medical technology and, as I then thought, the unreliable technology of international money transfers. I could only begin to imagine the family's frustration and anger, feelings they might be ready to direct toward me for having abandoned Mohammad in Boston.

I had had a dream the night before I left the States about a house where I had once lived in Chapel Hill, North Carolina. In my dream, the house's foundation had sunk and a wall had caved in. Someone had dismantled the stove, and its bolts were scattered helter-skelter along with pieces of the jewelry that had been stolen over that Valentine weekend. I woke up thinking of how the Boston plan had fallen apart. Surely, I would find a despondent and demoralized Mohammad when I got back to the West Bank. What kind of welcome could I expect?

When I finally made my way to the camp four days ago, the *ahlen wasahlen*s were multifold. They began, in fact, at the East Jerusalem bus station. I was sitting in the bus that would be taking me to Deheishe when I saw Mohammad's mother, a box of food on her head, about to board with Hala, Mohammad's youngest sister. Malka usually does her big shopping in Bethlehem, but nearby Beit Sahour was under military closure as a result of the tax war.[3] On this particular day she had come to Jerusalem instead. When she spotted me in the front of the bus, her shouts of surprise and joy were quickly followed by kisses and hugs. Hala sat on my lap and Malka had her arm around my shoulders all the way to the camp stop. When I arrived at the house, Naim told me he would have met my plane the week before but for the sealing off of the West Bank over the Yom Kippur weekend.

I was once again on a level plain where words were clear and feelings unobstructed. Anything I might have said about my earlier fears of rejection or my present feelings of relief would have been insulting or confusing.

Journal Entry/A week later, October 21   My computer is out of commission until I get a new adapter for it. Mohammad's problem won't be so easily fixed. He was admitted to Makassad Hospital yesterday, the day my low battery light came on and it was impossible to recharge it. Mohammad's liver is malfunctioning and he may have septicemia. Doctor Qurie says his situation is "dangerous."

Less than three weeks ago, he returned from Boston looking better than ever. His Hickman catheter had been replaced, and all the test results were excellent. He was wonderful when I saw him last week. Far from being demoralized, he was as feisty as ever, full of stories about visiting the aquarium and bringing his Boston friends up to date on the Intifada.

Last week I had concluded that everything was under control, that all of us could succeed in keeping him alive for the future transplant despite the way the last visit to Deaconess Hospital had ended. I was doing for Mohammad what I could no longer do for my son, whose separation from me seemed to have grown both geographically and emotionally. I could keep my own and Mohammad's world intact despite the rubble of demolished houses that littered the West Bank as well as my dreams.

Looking into Mohammad's yellow eyes yesterday made me angry. Someone had found a way once again to enter my house and disassemble my world. I had checked all the windows and doors to make sure they were securely locked, but I hadn't figured on the foundation itself giving way.

Journal Entry/October 24   Mohammad is recovering from emergency gall bladder surgery, and my computer is now fixed. I knew I hadn't lost Deheishe's welcome when I left the camp two weeks ago. Having found a smiling Mohammad this afternoon at Makassad, I can keep him off my Lost List as well. One day, maybe I can let go of the other losses. Freedom *soon*, Max Roach?

Journal Entry/November 6 I'm back from forty-eight hours in Deheishe Camp, and what I'd like to do more than anything else is go see Gene Hackman's latest spy movie, which is playing at the Edison, the West Jerusalem theater closest to me on the Egged bus line. I may still try to catch the seven o'clock showing, except it will be dark by then and maybe raining. So it looks like I'll be in my Sheikh Jarrah apartment for the rest of the day and night, decompressing from yesterday's events at the camp.

Despite how bad things are now at Deheishe, Mohammad wanted to spend his first day out of the hospital with as many of his family and friends as were available, not many now because of regular roundups and arrests of so many of the *shabab*. Those not already in detention are on the "Bingo" list and therefore in hiding. Rafat is back at Ansar III. Nidal and Hazem spend most of their time outside the camp.

Nidal, Naim, and I accompanied Mohammad from Makassad with an Abu Aker relative who picked us up in his truck about eleven o'clock Saturday morning. When we reached the stone factory road, Nidal left us when he found out from some small boys that the army was patrolling that side of the camp. But an hour or so after we arrived at the house, Nidal showed up along with Ya'coub and two others on the "Bingo" list. Scores of other neighbors—women, children, and older men—dropped in to welcome Mohammad with their *hamdililla allah salamtak*s (thank God, you have returned to us safe and sound), the greeting to those who have come back from the hospital, from prison, or from a journey. Saturday was a day of high spirits and, except for the sound of soldiers' boots as they made their rounds, the night was quiet.

Sunday morning, Mohammad waited for the barber who was supposed to make a home visit to shave him and cut his hair. At the family's urging, I agreed to stay for an early afternoon meal of one of my favorite dishes, *malfuuf* (cabbage stuffed with rice, bits of meat, garlic, and parsley and doused with fresh lemon juice), before leaving with Mohammad for the apartment in Bethlehem we have been renting for him since his first return from Boston, a "safe house" for just such hot periods in the camp.

The barber never showed up, and before we were able to eat the *malfuuf*, a six-man army patrol entered the house to look for wanted youth. Nidal and the others made a fast getaway as we delayed unlocking the front gate for the soldiers. We assumed they would leave when they found only Mohammad in the house. But on checking his identity card with their computerized list of numbers, they announced that he was "Bingo."

Undeterred by our, the women's, frantic words about his condition and Mohammad himself showing them his bandaged and scarred abdomen, the soldiers insisted on taking him away. I insisted on going with him, and we walked very slowly down to the Hebron Road fence, lately reinforced with zinc panels. We stood at one of the openings for about a half hour as the head of the patrol radioed first for an officer who arrived in a jeep and then for an ambulance that would take Mohammad to Bethlehem military headquarters.

There followed questions about the whereabouts of Nidal, Mohammad insisting that having himself just been released from the hospital, he had no idea of his brother's whereabouts. Shortly after that line of questioning, Mohammad walked over to a soldier who looked no older than a junior high schooler, took back his identity card, and began walking away. He motioned me to come along when I kept standing at the fence. Clearly, it was Nidal they were after, not Mohammad.

By this time, Mohammad's mother, who had changed from her housedress into her brown *thobe*, had reached the main road with a neighbor, and we walked back up the hill together, other neighbors along the way offering still more *hamdililla allah salamtak*s on both Mohammad's safe returns—first from the hospital and now from the soldiers. But the patrol was waiting for us when we arrived at the gate. The soldiers entered the house once again, this time to search for any incriminating material like Intifada leaflets, party materials, or anything combining the Palestinian colors of red, white, black, and green. Nidal, however, had done his job while we were gone. After his escape, so I learned this morning, he had made his way to the Bethlehem Red Cross office and two of their personnel were in the house waiting for us when we returned from the fence.

It was their presence and mine, I am quite certain, that kept the soldiers in line. They went through all the drawers and closets, but at least they did not smash the buffet and television or try to intimidate the women and girls. The junior high schooler even apologized for going through the family belongings: "I wouldn't like anyone to come into my house this way," he said to me as I stood in the back bedroom and watched him rummaging through the drawers.

The soldiers finally left and other neighbors began pouring in. But less than an hour later, another patrol came in and asked for "the sick boy."

If Nidal did not turn himself in by Wednesday, they announced, they would be coming back for Mohammad. Within minutes after their departure, Mohammad was on his way to Bethlehem and I was agreeing to stay on for another night "to protect the buffet," I said, if the soldiers decided to come back. I saw fear in Malka's eyes for the first time. I, too, was afraid—this time on the spot, not in my usual delayed and displaced reaction over the next day's or the next week's trivial irritation.

Except for the soldiers' setting fire to someone's book collection up the hill and their boots outside my window, the night was again quiet. I left early this morning, in the first car on its way to Bethlehem. Nidal was with Mohammad when I stopped at the apartment on my way back to Jerusalem. Far from being upset about the soldiers' threats, both of them were full of smiles. Mohammad, Nidal told me, was feeling part of things for the first time since the day he was shot. Of course, Nidal would not be turning himself in. "This kind of threat is normal for us," he said.

The rain has held off, and there is still time to make the spy movie. But I think I will get caught up on some ironing, which always brings me comforting thoughts about my grandmother and the smell of her apron.

Journal Entry/End of November Mohammad had to go back to Makassad the day after I stopped by his Bethlehem apartment. His incision had opened, and he was running a high fever. After his first confrontation with the army since the August morning he was shot, he was angry and depressed for the initial several days back in the hospital. In fact, his spirits were at their lowest ebb since an evening back in Boston when he had looked at a photograph of himself doing the *debkah*, the Palestinian folk dance he had led while he was a student at a private Latin Catholic school in Beit Sahour.

"I'll never dance again," he had sobbed. It was the first and last time I saw Mohammad cry. It took another week in Makassad for his mood to lift, even with the prodding and joking of Issa, a nurse who had been close to his case from the very beginning.

Mohammad was discharged two weeks later and now spends most of his time in the Bethlehem apartment, where he will not be subject to the around-the-clock raids still being carried out by the army in its concerted effort to arrest all the youths on its wanted list. When he is not watching kung fu videos, he is receiving scores of visitors who stop by to pay their continuing respects to the West Bank's "living martyr." Nidal is still on the run.

The high cost of living: other visits to Makassad

I was "shot" on my way out of Makassad the day after Christmas, 1989. My young assailant and I passed one another in the courtyard outside the hospital. He hugged the wall on the narrow walk, shoulders hunched and arms folded in front of him. As I approached the steps going up to the roadway, I heard him make the abrupt *dtuk-dtuk* of a soldier's automatic rifle, as good an imitation as the young boys his age make in Deheishe when they play *jesh* and *shabab*, soldiers and youth, the former with their long sticks of wood and the latter with cloth bands around their heads, Che Guevara style. I reeled and pretended that I was hit. When I turned around smiling, he shot me solemnly a second time. It was not a game. I just happened to be the first Westerner who had come within his range that morning.

To pull myself out of a holiday slump, I had been distributing red lollipops to a few of my favorite patients. They included Sabah, age fourteen, and her twelve-year-old brother, Mansour, who were injured along with seven other members of their family when an antitank grenade exploded in their courtyard in Hebron. Sabah's legs were shattered from the knees down; Mansour lost his right hand, his right eye, and parts of both legs.

When I got to his room, Mansour was sitting in the wheelchair that a younger brother, the one who slept alongside him every night, pushed up and down the hospital corridors on their daily rounds. I gave Mansour the rest of the bag of candy and asked him, *min fadlak* (please), to pass them out to his friends. He gave the first lollipop to the seventy-eight-year-old man, a beating victim, who always winked at me from his bed across from Mansour's. Everyone was laughing when I left. Mansour was beaming.

By the end of 1989, Makassad had become a third home for me, after Deheishe Camp and the Arab-style apartment I had been lucky enough to find in the Sheikh Jarrah neighborhood of East Jerusalem. My regular hospital visits had begun with Mohammad more than a year before, when I saw him for the first time from the doorway of the intensive care unit and assumed that he was fast on his way to martyrdom. I visited him daily during the month and a half he spent at Makassad following his return from Boston and subsequently during his recurring bouts with infection.

It was during that early month that I met the young teenagers Suhaib and Marwan. Suhaib was the first serious Intifada casualty in East Jerusalem; Marwan was an early casualty of the aggie-sized round bullet that had been introduced into the Israeli arsenal for crowd control. He was from Gaza. Mohammad, by then a national hero, had spent time with both of the boys while his fistulas were healing.

Marwan was shot on January 5, 1989, in what his cousin described as "the most quiet place in the Gaza Strip." On the Thursday afternoon of the shooting, Marwan was on his way home—"eating a sandwich," his cousin reported. A group of children scurried off as a military patrol approached the area. As Marwan was hurrying toward his home, a soldier, without provocation, shot him in the back of the head from a distance of fifteen meters.

The youth was taken first to the local UNRWA clinic and then to Ahli Hospital in Gaza City. From there he was transferred to Makassad Hospital, where doctors dared not remove the bullet for fear of further damaging his brain. They sedated him both to allow time for the swelling to subside and to keep him still, since the round bullet was sliding back and forth along the path of its entry. Regular forceps, unable to grab the bullet, only pushed it back through its pathway. Marwan's neurosurgeon eventually devised a special instrument. He attached a magnet to the end of a stick so that the lead core of the bullet could be attracted out of the brain. The doctor would go on to use the simple instrument on other such brain injuries.

In the meantime, an Israeli human rights lawyer, Avigdor Feldman, published an article about Marwan in the January 20 issue of *Hadashot*, one of several Hebrew-language newspapers providing fuller coverage of the Intifada than the local Arab papers, which have to conform to stricter rules of censorship. Feldman entitled his article "Marwan Learns to Live with a Marble in His Head." Part of it read:

> Let us say that you are Marwan Maghari and a metal object weighing
> 20 grams and covered with very thin plastic is in your brain. It looks
> like a marble from a children's game. . . . You lie there in Makassad
> Hospital and you are all alone. You would be consoling yourself, if the
> consoling center in your brain were not damaged. After all, you were
> privileged to be shot by an officer. Those shot after you will get the
> bullet from only a first sergeant, a second sergeant, or simply a regular.

Your eyes are closed. You may be singing a Palestinian song, and images pass through your brain. Your doctors are not promising you a rosy future. They say if they get the bullet out, other cells in your brain may be damaged. Your destiny may be to live with a marble in your head.

The writer and neurologist Oliver Sacks . . . talks about a music teacher who could live a normal life except for one thing: he couldn't differentiate between his wife and his hat. . . . . Dead areas in the brain lose the ability to identify things that are not where they are used to being placed.[4]

Suhaib Abu Ghosh was injured twelve days after Marwan, on January 17, the victim of severe beating by East Jerusalem's border police who claimed that the sixteen-year-old fell from a wall while trying to escape. A Makassad surgeon found plastic bullet fragments in his head, and eye-witnesses testify that the police prevented two Palestinian doctors from coming to the boy's aid. Passersby who tried to help were shot with rubber bullets.

After Suhaib was out of intensive care, he remembered being shot at four times and then beaten. On my last visit, he spoke only in a whisper, constantly agitated, his eyes full of fear. "Were he fifty years older," I wrote in the human rights center's February *Update*, "one might mistake him for an Alzheimer's patient."

An English-language broadcast on Radio Israel two months later brought Suhaib back into my mind. The announcer was reporting on the Ninth Jerusalem Conference of Mayors, which had just ended. The day before, on April 10, 1989, a Palestinian had been shot at close range by a man in army uniform. Twenty-six-year-old Khaled Shawish had been sitting with friends on the grass just outside Jerusalem's Old City Jaffa Gate following the evening Ramadan meal when the uniformed man opened fire.

In the closing session of the conference on the night Shawish was killed, Jerusalem's mayor, Teddy Kollek, had told the mayors, most of them from the United States, that "despite the months of stress and strain [because of the Palestinian uprising], Jerusalem remains a vibrant, functioning, and exceedingly beautiful city." He went on to emphasize the strong unity that continued between the Jewish and Arab sections of the city.

A visiting mayor from Schenectady, New York, echoed Kollek's sentiments in the interview that ended the radio report I listened to that morning. After all, she asked, what American city escapes problems, even occasional acts of violence against its citizens? One must remember, she went on, that an international piano concert had taken place in Jerusalem that week, evidence enough that a rich cultural life was going on in the middle of the troubles.

I listened to the broadcast in my Sheikh Jarrah apartment, just as cozy in its way as the American-style studio apartment I had lived in on the other side of Jerusalem during my research year in 1986-87. Kitty-corner from Mayor Kollek's house, the earlier apartment was in Rahavia, an older residential neighborhood designed in the 1930s by Berlin architects to create something reminiscent of the Bauhaus Germany they had left in their escape to Palestine.

My seventy-two-year-old Rahavia neighbor, Hilde, was a Lithuanian who came to Palestine in 1937, a few months after I was born. She married Hans, a German lawyer who prepared himself as a baker in order to join the emigration preceding Hitler's invasion of Poland. Hilde's father and brother stayed behind and were gassed at Dachau. Her sister survived a concentration camp to emigrate eventually to Canada. Most of the older residents of Rahavia had similar stories to tell. Their collective tragedy was strangely memorialized for me in the neighborhood's deco touches: rounded balconies on rectangular structures, geometrical grill-work around windows and doors, all of them features of Arabic culture, as I later learned on my first visit to Cairo.

On that perfect April morning some two years later on the Arab side of the city, I could almost understand the sentiments of the mayor from Schenectady. I, too, had at one time been under the spell of Teddy Kollek's Jerusalem. It did not surprise me that she was taking leave of this city of cities with the music of Chopin in her head.

But there was another Jerusalem, its name *Al-Quds* in the language of Arab residents like Suhaib. The sound of his silent scream filled my head once again as I listened to the broadcast. I recalled the look in his eyes, the look of a cornered wild animal that I saw in my mother's eyes the last time I saw her in the Western Pennsylvania nursing home where she was dying of Alzheimer's disease.

One of the last times I visited Suhaib before he was released from Makassad, he had given me an "urgent message" in English for Prime Minister Yitzhak Shamir. "The children of Palestine carry the flag," he had said. On that afternoon in early February, the international piano competition in the mayor's Jerusalem was several months away. For Suhaib, it would be taking place on another planet.[5]

I often visited Makassad Hospital with yet another of the human rights center's field-workers. A man in his late thirties, he was one of the thousand-plus political prisoners released in 1985 as part of an exchange with Israel. A torture victim with a metal plate in his head, he had served seventeen years of a life sentence. He was now married and the father of twins. On one of our visits, we saw fourteen-year-old Ali, who was injured in the Nahalin massacre in late spring 1989. The bullet that entered Ali's right side exited on his left, destroying one kidney and damaging the other. It also passed through his spinal cord, and he was now paraplegic.

In addition to Ali, we saw several brain-dead teenagers still in the intensive care unit. The hospital wanted to give the extended family time enough to make their farewell visits and to arrange ways to bury the bodies without army interference. One of the teenagers, another Ali, was from Deheishe Camp. He had been shot in the head at close range with a rubber bullet, then beaten and dragged face down through the street next to the Abu Akers'. Another of the intensive care patients had had his right index finger shot off as he made a victory sign. The same bullet went on to lodge in his brain. I will always remember the comment the field-worker made as we left the hospital that day: "Life is difficult," he had said as we climbed the steps to the roadway, "but it is not impossible."

I found I could not stay away from Makassad Hospital. It was not just that I wanted to witness close up the human cost of the uprising. For my own sake, I needed to see the wheelchair rounds of a laughing Mansour as well as the hands that touched and tried to heal the wounds: the knowing hands of Leila, the blind physical therapist, and the ever-so-caring hands of Issa, Mohammad's nurse, with whom I talked about the Palestinian writer Ghassan Kanafani between bandaging and hypodermic needles. Kanafani wrote about the camp children who walked "miraculously between the shots," those who were luckier than Marwan, Suhaib, and the two Alis.

"Kanafani is our bullet," Issa had said to me, "our commando without a gun." The boy who "shot" me outside the hospital was about the age of Kanafani's son, Fayiz, when he found out he was a Palestinian.

Celebrating survival

Journal Entry/August 5, 1989   The crunch is on to finish the next *Update*. Writing about the month's shooting, beating, and teargassing victims is my regular assignment at the center. I always find ways to procrastinate, not only because I find it painful but also because it has become so damnably routine. There were thirty-eight deaths in July. Fifteen of them were children, including a ten-month-old baby who died from teargassing. Most of the others were teenagers like Mohammad. If you adjust for the difference in populations, a ratio of 163 to 1, thirty-eight deaths in the Occupied Territories would be like 6,194 deaths in the United States.[6]

Tomorrow, Deheishe Camp will be throwing a party to celebrate Mohammad's first year of survival. A Lazarus come back from the dead, he has become a symbol of his people's struggle and their hope for life beyond occupation.

Journal Entry/The next day, August 6 I arrived in Deheishe this morning, carrying the gift Mohammad had requested: a bottle of Adam aftershave cologne—named after my son, I joked with him. When I went in the house, I discovered that Malka and Hala had gone to visit relatives in Amman for a week or so. Without Malka's cooking, the celebration would be on a less grand scale than I had expected. Even at that, things were unusually quiet. No one was in the front of the house.

On my way back to the veranda, I found Naim stretched out in the bed I usually sleep in on my overnight stays with the family. He showed me a note from a Bethlehem doctor, scrawled in English. The only words I could make out were "urgent" at the beginning and "infarction," a medical term I knew was connected with heart attack, at the end. "I need to get to Makassad," Naim told me. Had the past year put that much strain on him?

I proceeded to the veranda, where I found Mohammad looking very glum. First off, I thought he was upset about his father, but it turned out he was running another high fever. In fact, his temperature was a half point higher than the one that landed him in the hospital only a few weeks ago. Clearly, there was to be no celebration that day.

I spent the next three hours, first, in persuading Mohammad that he had to go to the hospital with his father and, once his older brother Nidal and I got him there, persuading him to stay. Trying to imagine what he must be recalling from a year ago, I had the doctor translate to him something like the following:

"Look, Mohammad, this time you are *walking* into the hospital, not being carried. And you have a future to think about. It is not only your

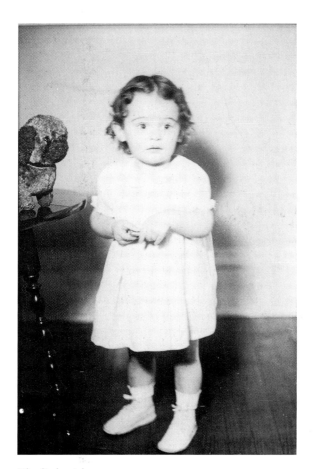

The little girl

Deheishe in 1956, when it was still a camp of tents. UNRWA later built concrete-block modules for the families who had fled 36 villages in the region. (Courtesy Deheishe Camp UNRWA office, photographer unknown)

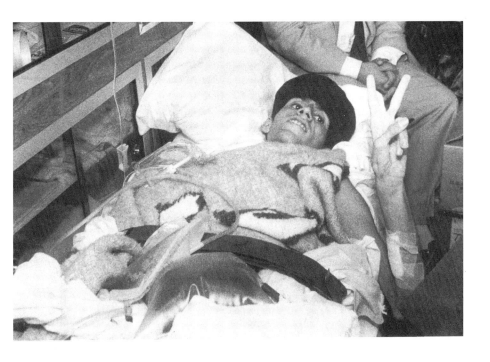

(*Above*) The "living martyr" arrives in Boston. (Courtesy The *Boston Globe*; by permission) (*Right*) Author with Deheishe children.

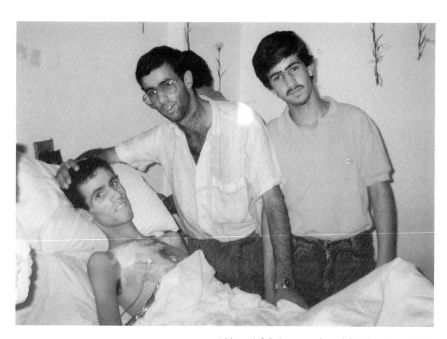

(*Above*) Mohammad and his brothers Rafat and Hazem at his seventeenth birthday celebration (September 1988) in Makassad Hospital before he went to Boston for medical treatment. (*Left*) Eighteen-year-old Mohammad "playing soldier" a few months before he died, in October 1990. (*Below*) Studio portrait that Mohammad, like most active *shabab*, had taken in case he became a martyr (the photos were used in the martyrs' funeral posters). This portrait, the model for the charcoal drawing, was later hung above Malka's place in the women's mourning salon.

(*Above*) Mohammad (center) with friends (at the homecoming celebration after he had returned from Boston, March 1989). (*Top, right*) Charcoal portrait of Mohammad in the Abu Aker courtyard garden. (*Bottom, right*) The charcoal drawing of Mohammad made for his homecoming party in March 1989, hung against a banner in the colors of the Palestinian flag as part of the mourning rituals for a martyr. The smaller photo is of Rufeida Abu Laban, another Deheishe martyr.

(*Above*) Malka (left) dancing in the street at Mohammad's homecoming. (*Left*) Mohammad's grandmother, the *hajeh*. (*Below*) Naim (left) and Nidal, who had just been released from Ansar III, embracing in a corridor of Makassad Hospital before Nidal sees Mohammad for the first time since his brother's injury (October 1988).

(*Above*) Naim, Malka, and a friend at Mohammad's crypt; neighbor Joffer is in the foreground. (*Below*) Malka (center) and two other women at Mohammad's grave. The Palestinian flags were later moved by the army.

(*Above*) Nidal in his wedding procession, holding a Palestinian flag in his right hand and a flyer about Mohammad in his left (September 1993). This was the first time a Deheishe groom carried a flag so openly (before the signing of the Oslo Accords). (*Left*) Mohammad's nephews Mohammad Rafat and Mohammad Nidal, living memorials to their martyred uncle (December 1994).

own future you must take good care of. It is the future of Deheishe and of all your people, because you have become their symbol."

Mohammad finally agreed to stay, but, as I learned a bit later, it was because his old room at the end of the surgery corridor was available once again, not because of my inspired words.

Nidal and I finally said good-bye to father and son, the former in the coronary care unit, the latter in the room where he had somehow survived a year ago, first to celebrate his seventeenth birthday, then to get lifesaving treatment in Boston. When we got back to the camp, the anniversary cakes began to arrive. To ensure their uninterrupted flow, Nidal told his friends that Mohammad was asleep behind the closed door of his bedroom. His younger brother Hazem had covered a pile of clean laundry with a blanket and, at his request, I took a picture of him sitting on the bed beside his "brother."

By the time I left the camp late this afternoon, five cakes had arrived and more were on their way. I laughed to myself all the way back to Jerusalem.

Journal Entry/A week later, August 13   A reading on BBC this morning from that section of *A Tale of Two Cities* about Madame Defarge, who patiently sat knitting during the French Revolution. The story reminded me of Malka's sister-in-law, who spends much of her time doing the traditional Palestinian cross-stitch. I admired two long dresses (*thobe*s) she had made for Malka and Nida'. On the lower back panels of both dresses, the sister-in-law had used the design that designated the area from which the family had originally come. Both Malka and Naim had been born in Ras Abu Ammar, a village in the Jerusalem District that is now part of the state of Israel. Naim remembers riding in the bed of a truck on a hot August day, forty-one years ago this month. Then a four-year-old, he had sat on top of the household goods that his family had managed to collect in their escape from the Jewish Palmach. Along with tens of thousands of other refugees, the Abu Akers headed southwest, first to the village of Irtas and then to Doha, both of them adjacent to Deheishe, where Naim eventually settled with Malka in 1967.

Married a year before the June War, he and Malka decided to rent a small place in Deheishe, by then "home" to Malka's family, since Naim's family compound in Doha was steadily expanding. As the next-to-youngest brother, Naim was almost last in line for diminishing space in the family compound, where four of his five brothers and their wives were living and beginning their families. When the June War broke out, most of Malka's family left for Amman except for an aunt who stayed on with Malka's mother and father. Buses supplied daily by Israel took thousands to Jordan, where Malka and Naim planned to join the rest of the family until they received a message from one of Malka's brothers to stay put in the camp, the situation on the other side of the Allenby Bridge reportedly not much better. The Deheishe population, numbering nearly eight thousand according to a 1991 UNRWA report, was twice that figure, nearly sixteen thousand, before the outbreak of the 1967 war. Once the war was over in six short days, no buses were provided for a return trip. There was no right of return for Malka's family or for thousands of other Deheishe residents who left in 1967 after many of them had fled their villages twenty years earlier.

Instead of going to Amman, the couple moved over to Malka's family compound with their recently born twin girls, who were seventeen days old when the war broke out. The babies died within a week of one another when they were less than a month old; Malka's breast milk dried up under stress, and they were unable to tolerate the powdered substitute supplied by the Red Cross. The second set of twins, Nidal and Rafat, were born the following year. Hala, the last child, was born in 1982, four months before Israel's invasion of Lebanon. Four years later, Malka and Naim and their six children along with Malka's mother would be moving into the new quarters they built on top of the concrete-block refugee quarters.

Malka had shown me the dresses her sister-in-law was cross-stitching before Malka went off with Hala to visit her brother and two sisters in Jordan. Through a series of gestures, she managed to communicate the fact that the sister-in-law had embroidered part of one sleeve during a raid that soldiers had carried out in her Doha house. Like Madame Defarge, she too had gone about her daily business in the middle of a revolution. In the process, she was able to celebrate the survival of the family birthplace in the Jerusalem region, if not in fact, at least in symbolic cross-stitching on the back of two Palestinian *thobe*s.

Chapter 4

Through the Looking-Glass in Cairo

Sunday morning, April 8, 1990

The Jerusalem-Cairo tour bus made its way at nearly midnight through Ramadan crowds still strolling in the brightly lit Cairo streets. What a contrast to the dark and empty streets of East Jerusalem after sundown! I booked into the Salma, the hotel where I stayed on my first trip to Cairo in December 1986, when I had had to vacate my Rahavia apartment for its owner, who had come to Israel for her Christmas break from Radcliffe College. At noon yesterday, Diana, an Australian friend who is teaching English in Cairo, picked me up at the hotel and brought me, four pieces of luggage, and my new Italian straw hat to her apartment in Zamalek, one of the city's more prosperous neighborhoods, where tourists can dine on French cuisine in outdoor cafés and shop for Egyptian cotton ensembles in the boutiques that line its little alleys.

My first foray this morning was in search of an English-language newspaper. I ended up buying three, one published here, the others in Kuwait and Saudi Arabia. One of the morning's headlines announced that Israel was preparing for war against Iraq. Two papers featured President Hosni Mubarak's response to Saddam Hussein's recent speech about his willingness to destroy half of Israel with the binary chemicals he can now deliver by guided missile. Saddam's saber-rattling, the Egyptian president maintained, was an understandable reaction to growing Western antipathy against Iraq and its recent execution of a British journalist, a former Iraqi citizen, accused of spying for Israel. This morning the BBC announced the U.S. expulsion of an Iraqi representative accused of abusing his diplomatic privileges. Could the Arabs be right in suspecting that the West is building up a case against Iraq so as to justify another attack like the 1981 Israeli air strike against the Osiris reactor in Baghdad?[1]

Last night I had a buffet dinner at the Nile Hilton with Jamil, a young Chicagoan of Syrian extraction who spent the past year in a West Bank damage-control program established by UNRWA during the first year of the Intifada. Jamil and other internationals like my Canadian friend Michael attempted to monitor activity in West Bank and Gaza refugee camps in an effort to reduce the number of confrontations between soldiers and residents. Jamil and Michael often stopped by the Abu Akers' when they were assigned to the camps around Bethlehem.

A friend of Jamil's here in Cairo has arranged a tour of museums and historic sites, but Jamil is having trouble gearing down. "I don't give a damn right now about pyramids," Jamil said to me. We ended the evening with a walk along the Nile, singing show tunes from *Finian's Rainbow* and *La Cage aux Folles*, which, more than the treasures of King Tut, proved an effective way of steadying the nerves.

Tomorrow I begin my six-week intensive course in Egyptian colloquial Arabic, the ostensible reason I have come to Cairo. What I really want to do is find money so Mohammad can go back to the States with me for his yearly checkup in Boston. The doors of New England Deaconess Hospital will remain closed until an outstanding charge of nearly $70,000 is settled.

Wednesday morning, April 11

On Monday I went to my first language class and last night met a possible money source—a doctor who heads the Palestinian Red Crescent Hospital in the Heliopolis neighborhood of Cairo. The hospital was established soon after the PLO exodus from Lebanon in 1982. I met Dr. Fathi at a reception he had arranged in honor of a Norwegian medical delegation who want to set up a joint program with the hospital. A friend of my Australian hostess, he had invited her to join them. "Dr. Fathi likes women," Diane said to me; "you should feel free to tag along."

Dr. Fathi happens to be the brother of Yasser Arafat. I was able to talk with him in his office down the hall from the reception parlor once the

Norwegians had been introduced and the guests had begun eating. Our conversation was brief, but I think I was able to communicate my credibility and concern. Adopting the blunt and somewhat poetic style of speech I have come to associate with Palestinians, I told Dr. Fathi that Mohammad's case was "inside my heart, even though I am outside Palestinian politics." We agreed to meet again soon—to "get down to brass tacks," I said. We need to take advantage of the widespread international interest in the case and, if possible, set up a trust fund for the long-term medical supervision Mohammad will need, especially if he gets the transplant. In the meantime, Dr. Fathi promised to wire "a Palestinian office in Washington" to get things moving. I assumed he meant Roots, the Palestinian-American organization that had been helpful at the time of Mohammad's initial hospitalization in Boston.[2]

Friday evening, April 20

I spent most of the afternoon with Dr. Mustafa, an Egyptian cardiologist whose name and telephone number Naim gave me before I left for Cairo. "A good man," he had told me. "Be sure to call him." In the winter of 1988, Mustafa had visited Mohammad at Deaconess Hospital during his month-long special training in laser heart surgery at Massachusetts General Hospital.

Mustafa picked me up in his blue air-conditioned Mazda in front of Diane's flat at 11:30 a.m. A large, muscular man with close-cropped hair, he was dressed all in white as though he had just come out of surgery. Friday, however, is his day off from his private clinic and the National Heart Institute, the "top heart center in the Middle East from Teheran to Rabat," he told me. Mustafa is also the personal physician of an Egyptian cabinet minister.

I asked him how he happened to hear about Mohammad when the two of them were in Boston. He said word had come by way of Lebanon, where, for six months, he had been a volunteer fighter back in 1975. He had been a fighter, he said, before he had become a doctor. He then told me to keep my own Palestinian connections to myself while I was in Egypt: "It would not be safe for you if the wrong people find out." I began to feel a little like Diane Keaton in *The Little Drummer Girl*.

The cinematic feel became stronger when we stopped off at the apartment of "an old friend" to deliver a stack of medications that Mustafa picked up at a pharmacy on the way. The friend was a rich Saudi who was visiting Cairo for two weeks. He was sitting at a coffee table covered with bottles of Pepsi and 7Up, along with a nearly empty bottle of Johnnie Walker and two opened packs of cigarettes, Cleopatras and Marlboros. Ramadan is no time for smoking; for the strict Muslim, no time is a time for drinking alcoholic beverages.

A small-boned man, the Saudi was also dressed in white—not Mustafa's trousers and overshirt, but a traditional *jalebeya* and skull cap. The Egyptian attendant who had answered the door was in a grey overshirt and matching pants. A woman in a long printed cotton dress and floral hair scarf—"his servant," according to Mustafa—served me a 7Up.

The first words the Saudi addressed to me were about a Lincoln Continental. He wanted to know the price of a limousine equipped with bar and television set, assuming, it would seem, that any American would have the price ready at hand. Or perhaps he assumed that an American woman like me would hold a certain image of a Saudi Arab and wanted to play on it. Whatever the case, I told him such cars were out of my class. To hide my uneasiness and, foolishly, to keep the conversation going, I told him that I would be willing to deliver one to him if he were willing to send me a round-trip ticket to Riyadh. As if on cue, he next turned the Hollywood-style conversation to the subject of women. Did I know any he could meet during his visit to Cairo? He would pay good money. Sensing my growing unease, Mustafa wished his friend well during the rest of Ramadan and moved toward the door.

When we got back into the Mazda, Mustafa told me his friend would most likely be willing to pay all of Mohammad's medical expenses, "past, present, and future," if Mohammad could supply a beautiful woman. Mustafa then drove me to his clinic in the Mohandessin neighborhood, where we were soon joined by his wife and eight-year-old son, Hazem, who came down from their apartment above. The four of us set off to do some shopping for the feast days that would be following the end of Ramadan next week. It was Hazem's turn to be outfitted, the clothes for the two younger children having been bought already.

The serious talk took place at the dining-room table later in the afternoon when Mustafa's wife set out a four-course meal just for me: a clear soup, the first beef I had seen since coming to the Middle East, a tossed salad, and a fruit compote for dessert. She and her husband would be eating later, when the Ramadan daily fast could be broken. Sitting at the table with me, Mustafa told me that he was in a position to arrange for the treatment of Palestinians wounded in the Intifada. "Poor Palestinians from the camps," he said. "It is my humanitarian duty as a doctor. And my religious duty as a Muslim."

We talked in particular about Mohammad's friend Ya'coub, who needs surgery to replace the nine centimeters of urethra damaged by a bullet several months ago. Ya'coub is what Mohammad's mother describes as *zarungi*, the Arabic equivalent of someone who has chutzpah. Thin and wiry with tightly curled hair that he wears in a modified Afro, Ya'coub struck me on first seeing him as a guerrilla fighter straight out of the camps of Lebanon or the mountains of Nicaragua. Like Mohammad, he is regarded as special in Deheishe, not only because of his and his twin brother's activism, but also because of a family history of resistance that began with his father in the early 1960s.

Ya'coub is indeed a cocky young man. I witnessed this for myself when he passed by the Abu Aker house one late afternoon while I was sitting out on the front balcony. He waved at me from the other side of the garden wall. The next thing I knew, I was being pulled inside the house to get away from the tear gas fumes that had begun to blow our way from the intersection where I had just seen Ya'coub. It was there, above the military compound at the bottom of the hill, that Ya'coub took his stand against the soldiers who had motioned him to move on. With one arm akimbo, he had dared the soldiers to shoot, and they lobbed a tear gas canister in his direction. The family were chuckling as they raced to close all the windows. "There goes Ya'coub again," Mohammad's mother announced, herself *zarungia*.

There are other Ya'coub stories, but these I know from others. In recent months, an officer has offered a reward of two hundred Jordanian dinars, more than six hundred dollars, to one of Ya'coub's neighbors for information on his whereabouts. Being on the "Bingo" list, he rarely stays at home. This officer is well known in the camp. He, like Ya'coub, sports an Afro for which the *shabab* have nicknamed him Abu Negro, a name that he accepts with a certain pride.

Abu Negro has publicly announced his intention of shooting a member of every camp household, whether it be a youth, a child, or an old man. One story has it that Abu Negro claimed responsibility for the martyrdom of the three Deheishe residents shot on successive days in April 1989. According to Mohammad's father, Ya'coub had a confrontation with Abu Negro that comes right out of an American western. Late one afternoon during last year's Ramadan, Ya'coub rounded a corner and saw the officer some five yards ahead of him. Ya'coub stopped in his tracks and challenged Abu Negro to a man-to-man fight.

"Put down your weapon," curly-headed Ya'coub shouted, "and let's see who is the *real* Abu Negro."

The officer handed over his M-16 to a member of his patrol, which, with the youths accompanying Ya'coub, stood and watched as the two of them advanced toward one another, step by step. When the Israeli Abu Negro quickened his pace and his patrol began to aim their automatic rifles, Ya'coub and the others ran the other way. The point had been made clearly enough.

Ya'coub is tough, but he is now scared. He has been receiving conflicting reports from two doctors at Makassad: his own urologist warned him of the permanent incontinency and sterility that might result from the two-stage operation he needs, although the other urologist, the current director of the hospital, told him the procedure was free of such risks. I told Ya'coub to get another opinion from an Israeli doctor before he let anyone touch him.

Ya'coub and I had been in the middle of talking about other angles on his case just before I left for Cairo: whether an Israeli specialist, who would have access to the prostheses needed to avoid such scary complications, might do the surgery; whether such a doctor would be able to perform the surgery in an Israeli hospital even though Ya'coub, long on the army's wanted list, would be subject to immediate arrest; whether Makassad's director would give permission for an Israeli to perform surgery in their theater. We then talked about the possibility of using the hospital facilities of Neturei Karta, the orthodox Jewish group that refuses to recognize the state of Israel until the coming of their Messiah. This group flies a black flag, not the blue and white Star of David, on Israel's Day of Independence each year, and they have made monetary contributions to Palestinian hospitals during the Intifada.[3]

Dr. Mustafa believes Ya'coub's surgery can be done at a urology center in Monsura, a city of five million not far from Cairo that has been doing kidney transplants for many years. We agreed that he would begin investigating this possibility while I was back in Deheishe, where I have decided to celebrate the post-Ramadan feast next week. I will be bringing back a copy of Ya'coub's medical report. I will also bring back a copy of Mohammad's Boston bills, about which Mustafa says he has "some ideas."

As it turns out, Mustafa has connections not only with the Egyptian medical establishment but also with Israelis who would be able, he says, to arrange at his "special request" safe passage through Israel for a wanted Palestinian like Ya'coub. Giving no names, he spoke of a man who, together with his son, has had dealings with both Yitzhak Shamir and Shimon Peres. The father is in Mustafa's debt for a "past favor" and would be able, so Mustafa believes, to arrange a "secret way" for Ya'coub to get as far as the Egyptian side of the Rafah border. Mustafa himself could get Ya'coub from there to Cairo. Naim seems to be right: Mustafa is "a good man." Or is it, again, something out of Hollywood?

Tuesday, May 8

I finally arrived back in Cairo last night, more than two weeks later than I had planned. The Egyptian Embassy in Tel Aviv was closed for the feast days and I could not get my return visa processed. It looks like the time I missed will make it impossible for me to continue with the intensive Arabic program. But I was able to bring back Ya'coub's medical report, and Mustafa did some further investigating while I was gone. Having found out that Ya'coub needs a plastic surgeon, not a urologist, he has arranged for free treatment in a Cairo hospital. More than that, he has found a "better way" to get Ya'coub out of Israel.

The transfer, it turns out, can be arranged through the Red Crescent Society, the Arab equivalent of the Red Cross, rather than relying on subterranean efforts by Mustafa's Israeli contacts. He tells me that an Egyptian government minister can facilitate the process, if the Palestinian ambassador to Egypt is willing to write a letter to the Egyptian Red Crescent on Ya'coub's need for medical treatment in Cairo. His letter needs to accompany the Egyptian Red Crescent's authorization to the Geneva headquarters of the International Red Crescent. Within ten days of receiving the two documents, the Jerusalem Red Crescent headquarters would be contacted to schedule the transfer. Ya'coub could be in Cairo within the month.

Getting the official letter from the Palestinian ambassador is, for some reason, up to me. Maybe because, as Mustafa told me at our first meeting, Egyptians sympathetic to the Palestinian cause need to keep a low profile. Whatever the case, Mustafa gave me the name of the ambassador and the address of the Palestinian Embassy this afternoon. I will set out on my mission first thing tomorrow morning.

Back on the West Bank, May 22

Along with my passport, I took with me every piece of plastic I owned when I set off in a taxi that next morning to the quiet residential neighborhood of Dokki where the Palestinians set up their embassy after Yasser Arafat declared an independent Palestinian state in November 1988. I figured that it would take some doing to get by the heavy security I expected to find on the premises and very possibly in the entire area. When the driver stopped in front of a modest family-sized residence, I was at first incredulous. In view was a ragtag group of four Egyptian police, two of them smoking cigarettes and all of them on anything but full alert. The driver insisted that this was the address I had given and, after noting a Palestinian flag flying in the side yard, I got out of the taxi.

Without asking me to produce any identification, one of the policemen motioned me to the side door, which was open and unattended. Finding no evidence of life on the ground floor, I made my way up the stairs to the first floor, where, again, there was no one to be seen. I finally called out a "yoo-hoo" into the empty corridor, and a young man came from somewhere to greet me. When I told him I was there to see the ambassador, he led me to an unoccupied room before taking me next door to a second room, this one with a large desk and several chairs. I assumed it to be the ambassador's office, since there was a large photograph of President Arafat on the wall behind the desk and a Palestinian flag in the corner. A burly man in shirt, tie, and business suit soon appeared and introduced himself as the man whose name Mustafa had given me. Still no question about who in the world I was. I decided nonetheless to certify myself as a human rights worker on the West Bank who was involved in the widely known case of the "living martyr," Mohammad Abu Aker.

No particular reaction from the ambassador, so I moved on to the point of my visit. "I need a letter from you, in English," as I mistakenly and chauvinistically thought at the time, "to get help for a Palestinian named Ya'coub." After I explained how his letter would be used, he said he would be happy to supply it but the man who did his English typing was not at work that day. Without pause, I offered to do the typing myself if he could supply a typewriter.

Less than ten minutes later, I was sitting in front of an old manual Olympia typewriter that the young man who greeted me took down from a storage closet in yet another room. When I finished typing the letter, the ambassador signed it and added an official governmental seal, my first piece of official business with the newly declared state of Palestine. I joined him and a group of other men for a cup of tea and talk about the land from which they had been exiled in 1967 or 1948, when their respective families had moved to Lebanon or Syria or Egypt, where they had been living ever since. They had no doubt but that they would be returning soon to their own state.

When I later described to Mustafa the seeming naïveté of the young and as yet prebureaucratic government, he said, "While some things are very complicated, other things can be very simple." I'm not sure just what he meant or into which category my morning's adventure fell. I do know that by the time I returned to Deheishe Camp two weeks later, Ya'coub was recovering nicely from the surgery that was performed at West Jerusalem's Hadassah Hospital shortly after post-Ramadan feasting. As it turned out, the needed procedure was determined to be minor once more X rays were done. Costs were covered by UNRWA.

As far as we know, no wire about Mohammad ever arrived in Washington. I am back now on the first side of the looking-glass, where humor and endless patience have to substitute for undercover activity, where ordinary life under occupation has to substitute for Hollywood intrigue.

Empty waiting, endless watching

Not long after returning from Cairo, I spent four days under curfew at Deheishe, a strong curfew imposed after the mowing down of seven Gazan day laborers on the outskirts of Tel Aviv (Rishon) on May 20 by an out-of-uniform Israeli soldier. Palestinian response to the massacre—Black Sunday, they called it—was immediate and widespread. Angry spontaneous demonstrations broke out not only in Gaza and on the West Bank but in towns and villages inside Israel as well—in places like Nazareth, Taibe, Haifa, and Om el-Fahem. Thousands of camp Palestinians in Jordan tried to storm the American Embassy in Amman. Hunger strikes calling for United Nations protection of Palestinians started up around the world.

Time began to hang heavy in Deheishe by the second day of the curfew. Numberless cups of sweet tea, long hours of American sitcoms and Egyptian melodrama on television, and endless watching of the crisscrossing army patrols and groups of youths from the veranda's widescreen view of the camp did little to break the boredom.

On the third day of the curfew, an UNRWA refugee affairs officer drove up in front of the Abu Aker compound to take Mohammad and his dropper machine to the Bethlehem apartment so that his food supply would not be interrupted if the curfew went on for much longer. I considered escaping with Mohammad, but because of a general strike called by the Intifada leadership there would be no transportation from his place to Jerusalem. I would be just as stuck.

By the fourth day, even the sound of live ammunition had become an unremarkable part of the background noise, along with Hala's whining. Boredom was relieved only by the challenge of finding food to supplement the rice and lentils remaining in the Abu Aker larder. Hala and I sneaked out of the compound to gather grape leaves from a neighbor's arbor, the family's own arbor having been blighted by Naim's excessive spraying of pesticides that spring. Finding Malka's flour supply now depleted, we called on Um Azziz for a couple of rounds of bread she had baked in her outdoor stone oven (*taboun*) earlier that morning.

Sitting once again in the veranda late that afternoon, I knew I would have to go home soon—not to my Jerusalem apartment but to the home I had left in Western Pennsylvania when I went off to college. The endless watching in Deheishe was recalling me to the front porch on Jefferson Avenue where, during the empty hours and months of childhood and adolescence, I watched the passing of neighbors on foot and, eventually, the drag racing of classmates in souped-up Chevies and Fords. For how many years did I wait for something to happen? Immobilized these latter days by the sheer boredom that revolution could too often impose, I knew I had to go back home to face whatever it was I left behind in going to the other side of the world. Some parts of home were not as far away as I thought. It seems I brought them with me.

A final evening in the veranda

On my last overnight in Deheishe, Nidal was imagining what was happening at that moment in Ansar III, the tent prison in the Negev where four of his friends were awaiting release the next day from six months of administrative detention. "Khaled will be giving his lecture now," Nidal suddenly said to me. The ritual of leave-taking from the tent prison included a final speech from those on their way out. The speaker would be expected to present his views on the Intifada along with an evaluation of his time in the detention center. As well as commenting on new resistance tactics he might have learned, he would also critique his behavior: Did he help keep the tent clean or was he lazy? Did he do as much as he could to keep up general morale or did he complain too much? Was he careful enough around suspected collaborators or was his talk too loose?

Collaborators were an especially serious problem in prisons and detention centers, since those places offered the only chance for Palestinians to exchange ideas and information with *shabab* from other parts of the West Bank. While the Shin Bet made sure that collaborators were on the scene, Palestinian prisoners and detainees made sure they knew who was who. The local Palestinian leadership ordered some years ago that all prisoners keep their eyes down during roll call, Nidal told me, since catching the eye of a guard was one of the ways a collaborator would send signals to prison officials. Prisoners were also ordered by their leadership to keep shirts buttoned all the way up, as unbuttoning to various levels was another code for communicating with the guards.

"The prisoners often stage Ghassan Kanafani stories to catch out collaborators," Nidal told me. One of the stories they used was "The Child Discovers That the Key Looks Like an Ax."[4] The only thing Kanafani's Jabr family had been able to take with them in the 1948 flight from their former village in Palestine was the iron door key to their house. The oversized key would hang from the walls of a series of temporary shelters and finally from the wall of the UNRWA-built house in the Lebanon camp where they ended up.

The narrator of the story, a child himself when his family left their village, had almost forgotten how he had seen the shape of a small ax in the key until twenty years later, when his own son discerns the resemblance. At the very end of his account of the family's history of exile and loss, the narrator reports that his son, Hassan, shouted, "pointing with his finger to the key: 'Look. It looks like an ax!' "

Like the scalpel that Kanafani imagined cutting its way into his son's chest when the boy first discovered his identity as a Palestinian, the ax symbolizes the pain of loss even as it holds out the hope of recovery. The struggle will continue; the homeland will be born again and again not only in a son's recognition of a key but in such epiphanies of familiarity and ordinariness as unlock for the father his own lived meaning of the Palestinian struggle. In Arabic, the word for struggle is *nidal*, the name that Malka chose for her firstborn son.

"The play's the thing," Hamlet said, and Palestinian prisoners dramatizing Kanafani's story about the ax would try to test the real feeling of suspected collaborators. The man assigned to the role of Hassan must somehow communicate, besides the power of the struggle to continue against a better-armed enemy, the child/father's sudden and painful recognition of being a Palestinian. A collaborator, according to Nidal, could not possibly pull off such an assignment without exposing his true colors.

The four Deheishe detainees would now be listing their shortcomings, Nidal said, their failure to control tempers, to share food, to resist taking the largest glass of tea, to communicate enough with prisoners from other parties. And then they would submit to further criticism from their tentmates.

"The worst they can hear is news of their banishment from the party"—for serious breaches of the behavior code they were expected to observe during imprisonment—Nidal told me. This news would be communicated by prisoner leaders to leadership in the detainees' camps and villages, and, until their future behavior warranted reintegration, they would remain outsiders.

"In prison, a man can be seen for who he really is," Nidal said. The so-called leader who takes the largest glass of tea or dozes off during study periods will have to descend the ladder.

"We know our leaders by their work," Nidal said, "not by their clever speaking."

When I left Deheishe the following morning, Mohammad had already gone to join several friends who were trying to organize a small caravan of cars that would await the returnees at a designated meeting spot on the way back, where, Nidal said, they would have a picnic. If all went smoothly, the entire group would be in Deheishe by late afternoon. The four would then go to their respective homes and, for the next three days, they would be receiving their friends and neighbors coming with sugar and rice along with their *hamdililla*s. At the end of the week, Nidal hoped, they all would have an overnight reunion party in a safe place outside the camp. Those who had managed to stay out of Ansar III during the past six months would then be gearing up for their own anticipated detentions.

Nidal hoped that he would be able to stay out of prison this time around, "to enjoy the season's fruit," he said. The past year and a half, ever since his release just three days before Mohammad's first departure for Boston, had been his longest spate of freedom in five years. Instead of living one day at a time, he was, for the first time, allowing himself to glimpse a possible future. Now that he had managed to pass the final high school exams, he planned to make application to Bethlehem University, which might open again in the next several months.

"Everyone will be singing now," Nidal imagined toward the end of our evening conversation on the veranda. "Not loud, because the other tents will be asleep"—the tents where Fatah, Democratic Front, Communist, and Hamas supporters were living in their respective party groups alongside the Popular Front tent. Good-byes had already been said to the other tents during the day.

In what turned out to be our own good-bye session on the veranda, Nidal and I talked that night about what lay ahead for the youths preparing themselves to go back to Ansar III as the others were getting ready now to leave. Nidal said that the struggle would probably be a long one.

"It may take the next generation of strugglers to win our rights," he said. "But look at how things have developed. Look at the difference between my grandmother, content to stay quiet in her corner, my father, who just worries about Mohammad, and someone like Joffer." Joffer was an eight-year-old neighbor who joined every camp demonstration his legs could run to.

"We must believe in history," Nidal said. "And we must have a strategy, since this is what makes us different from the animals. It isn't enough just to live."

I would be returning home in two weeks with no flags of achievement. The martyrs' report I had been assigned to write for the human rights center remained unfinished. The autobiography workshop I had hoped to conduct for the center's field-workers never got off the ground. Cairo had turned out to be a never-never land. I would be leaving a difficult situation that only seemed to be growing worse after the Black Sunday massacre and the Palestinians' more recent retaliatory attack on the Tel Aviv beach, which ended the U.S. dialogue with the PLO. My government, it turned out, would be preparing for war against Iraq only a week after I got back. Having "just lived" for those two years seemed my sole accomplishment and, as Nidal had said, it was not enough.

PART II

THREE RETURNS

Chapter 5

First Return: Mourning a Martyr

We never really said good-bye, the Abu Akers and I. Malka and Naim had not yet returned from Jordan when I left Deheishe for the last time to resume academic work back in the United States. They had gone to Amman several weeks earlier to check into possible funding for Mohammad's next trip to Boston. As for Mohammad, Nidal, and the rest of the family, I left them in the usual way, as though I would be returning again the next week. There are as many Arabic expressions of leave-taking as of greeting, but we found ourselves unready to use any of them. I simply walked out of the house, Mohammad having left fifteen minutes earlier to take the last of a series of driving lessons in Bethlehem. As it turned out, Mohammad would be driving himself to Makassad Hospital when, three months later, he died.

The two of us were especially sad, because we had hoped that we would be leaving together for Mohammad's next checkup at Deaconess Hospital in Boston. But it was becoming clear that funding would not be ready in time. "The money is waiting for Mohammad in Amman," the family had been assured by a medical committee in Jerusalem; "it is only a matter of delivering final papers to the right offices." Malka and Naim had gone to Jordan, planning to return to Deheishe within a week or, at the most, ten days. Two weeks after they arrived in Amman, frustrating messages began coming back to Deheishe through Red Cross channels.

Key officials were out of the country, the messages indicated. No one knew just when they would be back at their desks. Time was running out. Mohammad would not be occupying the plane seat I had reserved next to mine.

But we came up with another plan: Mohammad could fly to Boston on his own when dispersal of the money was eventually authorized. After all, he had managed to stay out of the hospital since the previous October when he had had emergency gall bladder surgery. With luck, he could avoid further complications for a while longer. "I'll be there to say 'Ahlen wasahlen' when you step off the plane," I promised Mohammad. Luckily, there were no pressing medical problems when I boarded the TWA flight for New York on the morning of July 27, 1990.

In mid-September, Mohammad was rehospitalized for sixteen days. On learning from Nidal that there was suspected kidney involvement, I wrote Dr. Sahyoun at Deaconess Hospital to alert him to Mohammad's medical situation. "The family is discouraged and frightened," I told him. Since funding efforts in Amman continued to be unsuccessful, I inquired about the possibility of setting up a special fund through Deaconess. "I, personally, would like to make a $5,000 contribution to such a fund," I wrote. I then asked Dr. Sahyoun for the names of persons in the Boston medical community who, knowing of his own "personal interest in the case," might be willing to contribute to such a fund. "We must find a way to open the doors of Deaconess once again for Mohammad."

I ended my letter with a worry that had begun to gnaw as a result of mounting Palestinian support for Saddam Hussein, who was being portrayed as a second Hitler. Oil-rich Arab states like Saudi Arabia, now more than ever the clients of U.S. foreign policy, were cutting the funding upon which Palestinian institutions like Makassad Hospital had long relied. "Since Makassad's budget has been cut as a result of the Gulf crisis," I wrote, "I wonder how long they will be able to absorb the costs of Mohammad's food?" My question implied that a small-bowel transplant might be Mohammad's only chance to stay alive, for political as well as medical reasons.

Nine days after I sent my letter and two weeks before Mohammad's death, Dr. Qurie, Mohammad's Makassad surgeon, performed exploratory surgery to determine the source of his severe abdominal pain. Whether Dr. Sahyoun tried to intervene, I do not know. I do know that Dr. Qurie told me some twenty months earlier, in mid-January 1989, "I didn't interfere in Dr. Sahyoun's business when I was with Mohammad in

Boston, and I don't want him interfering in my business over here." Dr. Qurie had been angry about the Boston doctor's impatience at Makassad's delay in organizing Mohammad's nutrition supplies in time for his return from the United States to the West Bank.

From the time Mohammad came back from lifesaving treatment at Deaconess Hospital almost to the day he died, Dr. Qurie, keeping a very tight rein on the case, shared information with none of his medical colleagues. Whether his handling of the case can be attributed to extraordinary devotion, to the inflated ego of a surgeon, or to factional differences (he being a Fatah supporter), I cannot say. In the end, a Deheishe journalist and close friend of the Abu Aker family insisted that another doctor be brought to Mohammad's bedside when Dr. Qurie took his usual day off, less than two days before Mohammad died.

Less than a month after I sent my letter to Dr. Sahyoun, I received sudden word that Mohammad was back in Makassad, this time in the hospital's intensive care unit. According to a medical report faxed to Jim Graff, "signs of kidney failure might require dialysis." His blood gas level was "dangerously abnormal" and he was "bleeding from the mouth and gums." The report was sent to Jim by our mutual friend Heather Spears, who was back in Jerusalem to draw charcoal portraits of injured Palestinians.

I first met Heather at Makassad in September 1988, when, a month after Mohammad was shot, she had drawn a portrait of the then-dying teenager for her collection entitled *Children of the Intifada*. Heather was at Makassad to draw a second series, this time of the Palestinians injured earlier that month when the Israeli border police opened fire on thousands who had gathered to protect Al-Aksa Mosque from a Jewish group calling itself the Temple Mount Faithful. Entitling this next collection *Massacre*, Heather would be appending it with a final drawing of Mohammad, who underwent his seventh and last operation on the same day, October 8, that seventeen Palestinians were killed and hundreds injured.

Jim Graff called me on October 20. I immediately made reservations to fly over the next day. Mohammad died of kidney and respiratory failure the morning of October 22, twelve hours before I arrived. Once again, I had not said good-bye.

I got to the Mount of Olives Hotel, across from the hospital, about 6:30 that Monday evening. It had taken longer than usual to get from Ben-Gurion Airport since, with fewer arrivals in Israel during the Gulf crisis, taxis filled up more slowly. Tourism was drastically reduced by the highly publicized distribution of gas masks in preparation for Saddam Hussein's threatened chemical warfare on Israel. Jerusalem was especially tense in the aftermath of three Al-Aksa revenge stabbings the day before in Baka, a Jewish neighborhood south of the Old City and just off the road to Bethlehem.

A curfew that was clamped on Deheishe as soon as word of Mohammad's death reached Bethlehem military headquarters kept me from going out to the camp that evening. It remained in effect throughout the first week of my stay. The curfew did not succeed, however, in delaying Mohammad's burial nor in keeping thousands of area residents from attending it. As I learned later, Mohammad's body was quickly snatched from the hospital by a small group of *shabab* who hid it in Bethlehem until a grave site was prepared at the small martyrs' cemetery in a nearby village where Mohammad's body could be placed next to other Deheishe Intifada martyrs. Mohammad's funeral procession stretched all the way through the mountain between Deheishe and the village of Irtas.

I stayed my first night in the hotel, where I shared a room with Heather. Her note about Mohammad's death was waiting for me when I arrived. The next morning, I walked over to the hospital to look for one of the Deheishe *shabab* I knew would be waiting for me. I visited two youths who had been shot seventeen days earlier during a demonstration in the camp. Lutfi had been shot in the head by a rooftop sniper; Iman had been shot in the thigh when he tried to rescue his friend. The shootings had taken place on Nidal and Rafat's twenty-third birthday. Their cake, Nidal told me later, remained uneaten.

A regular visitor at the Abu Akers, Lutfi seemed to recognize me despite heavy sedation. He extended his left hand, his right side useless. After a *salaamtak* and greetings to his mother and father, I found Iman walking on crutches at the end of the orthopedic ward upstairs. It was there that Ziad met me, figuring I would be in the hospital since I had not come to the camp the night before. The two of us waited for another Deheishe resident, Yusef, who was supposed to be arriving with his car to take Iman's mother back to the camp. When no car came in the next hour, Ziad and I decided to make our way by public transportation, hoping that the checkpoints set up following the Baka stabbings would not make problems for Ziad or delay both of us.

Mish mushkeleh, no problem. We got off the bus at my usual stop, the gas station across from the stone factory, and under the curfew made our cautious way across rubble and then through neighboring courtyards. In the end, we ran fast across the one pathway where we might have met up with soldiers. But there were no patrols in sight. Continuing to run into the Abu Aker courtyard and up the stairway, I was breathless when I entered the salon. It was filled with women sitting on mats that covered the entire floor.

I made my way through the crowd to Mohammad's mother, who was sitting against the far wall. She was underneath a huge banner in the colors of the Palestinian flag: green, red, black, and white. At the top of the banner and wreathed in fresh flowers hung a photograph of Mohammad. When I left in July, it had hung above the doorway that led to the back section of the house. It was the photo that Mohammad had had taken more than two years before, as though in preparation for both "martyrdoms," the one he had survived and the one we were now mourning. Malka made room for me to sit down beside her.

In the sea of faces, I began to recognize the women who had so often greeted me at their gates over the two years I had been going in and out of Deheishe. In among them, I saw the women I knew at closer hand, Abu Aker relatives, friends, and immediate neighbors. They silently nodded at me without surprise as I scanned the room. I understood their simple message: "You were part of Mohammad's life, and you have returned for his death. Ahlen wasahlen, you are welcome." My own nod said in return, "This is the only place I can be at this time, with all of you." We needed no words.

No soldiers entered the house during the first week I was there. It was more the rule than the exception for the army to interfere in the mourning process, as I knew from all the reports on martyrs I had written. Interference ranged from confiscating flags and banners to teargassing, beating, and shooting the mourners. Clearly, the army had received orders to keep their distance from the house of this particular martyr.

But distance did not mean that the military was not in evidence. During the week of curfew, eight to ten soldiers were just across the road from the house. Most of them were lounging against nearby walls or sitting on ledges protruding from neighboring houses. Usually there were several on a roof directly across the way. And, after the first two days, an army contingent occupied the top floor of an unfinished house up the hill. They had draped a huge Israeli flag out a window to make sure their presence was duly noted by the family and the mourners. Late one afternoon,

another soldier registered his presence by throwing a bottle through the
open window of the Abu Akers' veranda. It broke into shards on the tiled
floor but luckily did not hurt anyone.

Normally, a curfew means that all residents must stay inside their own
houses; they are forbidden to come out into their walled courtyards to
hang out laundry or, in some cases, even to use outdoor toilet facilities.
But the soldiers stationed around the Abu Aker household knew they
could not stop camp residents from paying their respects to the family.
This curfew was intended to keep outside the camp in the early days
other West Bank delegations who would be coming in droves the following weeks: representatives from Popular Committees that had sprung up
or been strengthened during the Intifada, regional representatives of
Popular Front as well as other Palestinian factions, and groups of young
women and men from Jerusalem and Ramallah who brought their special
songs, slogans, and handcrafted wooden shields into which their respective factional logos had been burned. On the walls of the ground-floor
salon, these shields would join scores of others that twenty months earlier
had been presented to the "living martyr" on his homecoming from
months of hospitalization.

Stationing themselves so near the house, the soldiers gave the *shabab*
some target practice. Stones were hurled at them like clockwork to divert
their attention and to allow the youths to enter and leave the house un-
harassed. On one of the curfew days, I called up to a young soldier sitting
on Abu Mamoun's roof.

"Why are you sitting up there?" I asked.

"I'm trying to keep order," he answered.

"If you were not there," I said, "there would be no problem. No soldiers, no stones."

Later on in the second week, after the curfew had been lifted, a ten-
man patrol came to the door of the lower salon to confiscate the flags and
banners. This ground floor room, originally the salon of the UNRWA-
built structure on top of which the Abu Akers had built their newer and
more spacious house, was the official mourning space for the men. Unlike
the salon upstairs where the women sat on traditional floor mats, this
room was lined with fifty or more small schoolroom chairs that were distributed for wakes and weddings. At its center were several low wooden
tables covered with packets of cigarettes on a large tray, a combination of
American and Arabic brands, and a large thermos of the bitter coffee that
was served in the smallest of cups, bedouin-style. Joffer, the activist

neighbor boy, had taken it upon himself to serve the coffee and to wash the cups in a red plastic basin of water.

As in the women's salon, Mohammad's face was prominently displayed. Based on the upstairs photograph hanging above Malka, the downstairs rendition of Mohammad's face was a much larger charcoal drawing, executed in a heroic style that reminded me of illustrations in a copy of Ayn Rand's *Atlas Shrugged* I had surreptitiously read behind my French textbook in junior high. Its planes accentuating a strong chin and piercing eyes, the drawing was hung between two large banners in the Palestinian colors. Like the upstairs photograph, it showed only Mohammad's head and shoulders. In this larger-sized depiction, however, the base of the human features ended in roots that extended downward from one side of the shoulders to the other. The rootedness and uprootedness of the Palestinians were symbolized at one and the same time. Like many of the wooden plaques, the drawing had originally been made to celebrate Mohammad's homecoming in March 1989.

When the army patrol arrived about ten that night, the room was almost empty. By that time, the banners, plaques, and other mourning decorations had been taken down and put away. But they had been in full view of passersby earlier in the day, and the soldiers would have to know they were somewhere in the vicinity to be put up again the next morning. By this stage of the Intifada, mourning conventions were set and predictable. More than a thousand Palestinians had been martyred by October 1990—the equivalent of 163,000 Americans in terms of comparable communal impact.

Those still in the room when the soldiers came to the door included Akram, a man in his late twenties who had studied Hebrew over the course of a five-year imprisonment from which he and Nasser, whose brother was studying in the States, were newly released. Along with Naim, Akram was able to negotiate with the soldiers for more time. Their initial success, as Nidal told me, meant that the banners and flags would stay for the duration of the mourning period. His prediction was only half right. While those inside the house remained unconfiscated, the flags that were erected at Mohammad's grave site were removed by the army.

Akram was initially wary when he saw me in the house for the first time during those weeks, but embarrassing adulation replaced that original suspiciousness when he learned about my two-year role in Mohammad's life, a role that he both admired and envied. Akram had entered prison two years before the Intifada began and came out in its third year to discover that everything was different. Even the camp pathways had changed, and he literally could not find his way from one place to another. He admitted to me he had to rely on children to find his way around.

Negotiating with soldiers, making banners, and arguing points of Marxist dialectics with Mohammad's friends was Akram's way of staying close to this martyrdom, thereby catching up on what he had missed during his five years away from Deheishe, removed from a revolution that was reshaping Palestinian history as well as the camp's system of byways and shortcuts.

Over the course of my two-year residency on the West Bank, I had visited the homes of many martyrs in my personal effort to understand the Palestinian situation and as part of my assignment at the human rights center. In fact, three such visits during the early spring of 1988 made clear to me that, as I had put it to myself, I could not *not* return to Palestine after my research year in Israel. That spring, I had made a quick trip to Jerusalem on my university's semester break to see what I might be getting into if I came back. As part of my reconnaissance, I went to the homes of three martyrs in the company of Samir Abu-Shakrah, a lawyer with the Palestine Human Rights Information Center, and Khaled Abu Aker, a Jerusalem journalist and a distant relative of the Deheishe Abu Akers I would come to know five months later. The first two visits were to el-Arroub, a camp situated on the same road as Deheishe but further toward Hebron, where two friends had been fatally shot—the second during a demonstration following the death of the first.

The third visit was to the home of a young man who had been shot less than a week before the birth of his first child. We arrived only days after the birth of his son, and the young mother, obviously still in shock, was sitting against the wall staring vacantly ahead in an upstairs bedroom where the mourning women were gathered. The baby, small and quiet, was being held by its grandmother in the crowded little room. I was sitting on the Western-style bed with other women and, before I knew it, the baby was in my lap. I remember turning to the woman next to me, a nurse at Ramallah Hospital who could speak English.

"Here I am an utter stranger," I said to her, "and you entrust me with this baby."

I will never forget the exact words of her immediate reply: "When you are in an Arab house, you are never a stranger."

I thought about those words more than once during those weeks of mourning with the Abu Akers. Far from being a stranger, I was in fact the only person who moved freely between the upstairs women mourners and the downstairs salon where I could smoke with the men and exchange words with visiting local groups and foreign journalists. I also moved freely between the more youthful *shabab* and *benat* (young women). I was fascinated with the tasks they had defined for themselves and carried out with such dedication, especially the decorative work that belonged, it seemed, primarily to the young men.

All official activity took place within the rooms that normally constituted the public space in the household: the downstairs salon that was used only for official occasions and the two upstairs salons, the traditional one with floor mats and the Western-style room whose upholstered furniture and glass and chrome tables had been cleared out for the occasion. The long curtains in both upstairs rooms were tied up in large knots. Stripped of the decorative elements associated with everyday living and redecorated by the young men with the paraphernalia of mourning, these spaces became sites of continuing resistance and increased resolve: "Mohammad lives on as a symbol of the Intifada," insisted the banners and flags and songs.

Within these undecorated and redecorated spaces, everyday life was suspended, at least during the daily mourning hours. In the evenings, however, a semblance of ordinariness was resumed in limited television watching (only the news), conversations frequently punctuated with laughter, and late snacks of fruit and icy cold cucumbers.

Except for a single wreath that had been placed outside and above the front door, the first week's decorative activity was indoors: the placing, unplacing, and replacing of banners and flags, and the freshening of wreaths with flowers picked from little gardens on the way to the house each morning, the perennials in the Abu Aker courtyard being, in late October, in short supply. As I was on hand with a ready camera, taking pictures of the youths in front of the banners and beside Mohammad's picture was added to the other rituals.

In the second week, with the lifting of the curfew and in anticipation of West Bank delegations at last getting into the camp, outdoor decorating began in earnest. The young men erected three sets of palm branches—one pair at either side of the front door, one at the top of the stairs to the balcony, and the third at the foot of the stairs. Another form of outside decorating—the political decorating that takes place all year round—took place one evening that week. The outside walls of courtyards and houses were spray painted with political slogans. As usual, the spraying was done at night by a masked "commando." Army regulations allowed soldiers to shoot such persons on sight without warning. The writing was sprayed on a wall one house down the hill from Abu Mamoun's while I watched out Mohammad's bedroom window along with several of the *shabab* and *benat*. "Mohammad and Our Glorious Intifada will never die," the slogan read. The next morning, a neighbor was commandeered by soldiers to paint over it.

A third kind of decorative activity bridged indoors and out and was intended for the ears, not the eyes. This was the music played over loudspeakers that seemed to multiply as the days went on. As soon as the sun came up, the music started out with the chanting of the Koran. There would soon follow the rousing "Thouri, Thouri, Thouri," an Intifada war song, as some called it, and a favorite of Mohammad, who, after the injury that benched him from stone throwing, would play it on his car stereo after parking as close to demonstration spots as he could maneuver his white Fiat. Other, more melancholy, songs were beamed out to the camp from the Abu Aker veranda, one of them a martyr's song whose lyrics took special notice of the young man's small waist. During the playing of that song, a soldier shouted up from the pathway below the windows for a number to which he could disco.

As much as by the decorations themselves, I was fascinated by the constant maintenance activity of the young men, moving in small groups from upstairs to downstairs to adjust pictures on the walls, to add more tape to banners that were beginning to sag (using medical tape left over from Mohammad's supply), and to relocate the speakers for greater impact on the camp and the soldiers. There was always the lettering of new banners to be done in the evenings on torn strips of white cloth, often inscribed at the lower left corner with the Popular Front logo. These activities were carried out in Mohammad's bedroom even though it was crowded with furniture that had been removed from the Western-style salon to provide eating space for the immense amounts of food that arrived daily for the family and extended family.

Just as they took care of every other domestic need for the two weeks I was there, the young women tended to the food, receiving and sometimes collecting it from neighbors, keeping it warm, serving it, and then cleaning up afterwards. While the young men dedicated themselves to maintaining the official mourning spaces, the young women, like their mothers on a more daily basis, made sure that ordinary life continued as smoothly as possible at the margins of those official spaces.

Unlike the *shabab*, a core of whom stayed at the Abu Akers' throughout the two weeks, the young women rotated, each successive group staying twenty-four hours at a time. In addition to heating up the chicken and rice dishes that arrived sometimes twice a day, the young women cut up tomatoes and cucumbers for salads dressed with fresh lemon and parsley and made supersweet tea and Arabic coffee nonstop to serve the friends and neighbors, mostly women, who arrived by eight o'clock in the morning and stayed until the family began to gather for a late afternoon meal. The *benat* cleaned up after the hundreds of daily mourners with the dirt of the camp on their feet. They cleaned the kitchen and bathroom from top to bottom, inside cabinets as well as outside. They cleaned all the windows, taking them out of their tracks so that both sides were accessible. And, of course, they washed hundreds of tea glasses and diminutive coffee cups over the mourning period. All of it was honorable activity for them and an expression of their love for Mohammad. They moved through it with the zest of cheerleaders at a homecoming game.

The fact that both groups of young people stayed the night with the Abu Akers certainly added to the enjoyment of their respective undertakings. More modern than many of their village cohorts, the young Deheishe men and women, especially those who like Mohammad's friends were politically active, got to know one another quite well before marrying, in particular through their committee work. Top priority in choosing a marriage partner went to political compatibility, not kinship connections, as was largely true for their parents. But even with the increase in contact brought about by Intifada resistance activity, sleeping outside their homes was a novelty, particularly with nonfamily members of the opposite sex just down the hall. Only when their official activity was finished for the day and all the adults were in bed did the two groups begin to mingle. I could hear them from the room I shared with Mohammad's grandmother at the end of the hall. The sound of giggles surprised me the first night. It was too easy to forget they were teenagers, not just revolutionaries.

But I was not all that surprised by the joking among the aunts and uncles who spent most nights while I was there. Even Mohammad's mother joined in the laughter after the salon emptied of visitors. Tears flowed during the day, especially with the arrival of the old women who could still remember earlier mourning rituals that called for wailing and the rending of their clothes. But rituals had changed during the Intifada. The mother and other women friends were as likely as not to deliver resolute national speeches about other sons who would have to die for the homeland. "This is our life; this is 'Our Situation,' " they would assert, much like Um Nidal the first time I met her in Makassad Hospital when Mohammad was close to death.

Sweetness as well as fierceness filled those two weeks. Sweetness was literal on Thursdays when, carrying out Intifada mandate, sweets were served to all the mourners. In the early morning, huge pans of baklava, *mabroma*, and *baloria* came into the courtyard on the heads of the young women who even during the week of curfew had somehow made their way out of the camp to Bethlehem bakeries to pick them up and then sneak back in without being confronted by army patrols. Heaping trays sat on every surface, on the glass coffee table then in Mohammad's room as well as on every counter and table in the kitchen. More sweets than could be eaten by the family and visitors, they were packaged up the next day in pieces of brown paper, ten to the package, for Hala and her friends to deliver to families around the camp. Even within that stripped-down space, Intifada mourning was more like a wedding than a wake. Only on the occasion of a martyr's death did a wedding-sized crowd gather, a crowd like the one that a year and a half earlier had welcomed back Mohammad like a bridegroom.

There was even a sweetness about the three visits to Mohammad's grave site in the nearby village of Irtas, whose name is derived from the Latin *hortus* or garden. The first visit to Irtas was on the day after I arrived in the camp. I was awakened early by two of the aunts.

"Mohammad," they announced. "Irtas."

The small group of six women, and Naim carrying a bouquet of flowers, walked the stony mountain path from Deheishe to the cemetery located just below the village's elementary school. Overlooking a lush valley, the cemetery stands between a mosque on one hillside and the convent and church of the Sisters of Notre Dame de Jardin on the other.

On that first visit, Mohammad's crypt was still decorated with three flags, a tall one in the center and short ones fanning out on both sides. But the flowers on the wreath had begun to wither, and the political flyer was beginning to tear. The flyer was illustrated with the Boston photograph in which Mohammad was flashing the V sign and wearing my Basque beret. The morning was fresh and bright, and even more lovely was the spring-fed valley stretching out below the cemetery with its huge gardens said to be inspired by the biblical Song of Songs. After one of the aunts read the Koran in front of Mohammad's crypt, two village men drove us back to the camp.

Some of the *shabab* joined us on the other two visits to say hello to Mohammad. The young men watered the vines they had earlier planted in front of Mohammad's crypt and cleaned up the area around the crypts of the other three Deheishe martyrs. One of the youths pointed out the bullet-shattered, glass-encased photograph of Rufeida that her family had recessed into the cement that sealed her crypt. By the second visit, the three flags had been confiscated. But on the third visit, Naim installed a replacement in the pipe that stood on top of the crypt and tied around the pipe two of the palm fronds taken down from the stairway back in the camp. On leaving that last time, I was unable to say or do anything in the way of a clear good-bye. As I slowly backed away from the line of crypts, I found myself whispering "*Yella, ma'a salama*, OK, let's go," a casual phrase that Mohammad and his friends used on normal occasions of leave-taking. Nothing more (or less) than the ordinary could rescue me from a loss below words and beyond tears.

When I left once again for the States at the end of those two weeks, the good-byes were elaborate and profuse. I was no stranger in that Arab house nor, for that matter, a stranger in that Arab camp. I would be returning to Deheishe for the second time the following June to see how my friends had fared during the Gulf War and again the next October to commemorate with them the first anniversary of Mohammad's death. On that third return, I would also be watching the televised opening of Middle East peace talks in the midst of Deheishe's growing dismay about prospects for a just settlement. A Palestinian woman would be asking Faisel Husseini, a West Bank leader of the Palestinian delegation in Madrid, "How is it that you were willing to go to Madrid for so little after so many of our sons spilled their blood for a free Palestine?"

The woman could have been speaking for Mohammad's mother as well as for the mothers of Nasser and Rufeida, who by then were among the ten Intifada martyrs from Deheishe. The woman's attack continued: "Our sons have died, they have been shot and beaten, they have gone to prison, and you went to Madrid without our flag, without our national anthem, without our identity. How could you betray the blood of our children?"

Nasser and Rufeida were fatally shot a month after Mohammad's homecoming celebration. They were the second and third of three killings that took place under the wide curfew that was imposed following a massacre in nearby Nahalin when Israeli border police opened fire on villagers leaving their mosque after morning prayer.[1] The first victim was Mohammad's next-door neighbor; the second was one of his best friends; the third was a girl who had visited him in Makassad before he went to Boston. I wrote the following report on the triple killings for the Palestine Human Rights Information Center (PHRIC) *Update* of May 1, 1989.

Three Martyrs in Deheishe Camp

April 15th was the beginning of three days of killing in Deheishe Camp. The first of three martyrs, 23-year-old Imad Mohammad Qaraqe, was shot during a curfew that was imposed following the Nahalin massacre. On the second day of the curfew, Imad went up to the roof of his house to feed the animals. He was shot in the chest while standing somewhere between the straw pile and the animal pen. Within 20 minutes, friends were rushing him to Beit Jala Hospital when soldiers stopped the car. Imad died at about 3:15 that afternoon. He was buried in a nearby cemetery in the village of Khader. A large number of camp residents escaped despite the curfew to attend the burial. The next day, the [Bethlehem] military governor accompanied by a civil administrator arrived at the victim's house to say that Imad was not killed by soldiers but by a camp resident who possessed an illegal gun. They even suggested he may have accidently killed himself while playing with a handmade gun. On the third day, soldiers raided their house.

The next day, April 16, the second Deheishe Camp killing took place during a demonstration against the shooting of Imad the day before. 16-year-old Nasser Ibrahim Ali al-Qassas was shot in the back as he turned to pick up a stone. The bullet exited through his right lung, tearing it apart. While still under curfew, his friends carried him through the mountains to the neighboring village of Irtas. From there they drove him to Beni Hospital in Bethlehem, through back roads to avoid soldiers. He was then transferred to Makassad Hospital where he died in surgery. Youths hid his body in Khader until the next morning when hundreds of residents broke the curfew to attend his burial. The third Deheishe victim was shot on the way back from the cemetery.

Nasser's family has a long history of resistance. His 60-year-old father has been arrested three times during the uprising and still has the marks of beating on his face. His mother has several times been taken to the Russian Compound in Jerusalem for interrogation. Nasser's older brothers have been imprisoned many times, one of them for a year and a half, another for two one-year administrative detentions. His younger brother was teargassed and beaten after soldiers killed his chickens.

Rufeida Khalil Ahmad Ali Abu Laban, the day following, was the third martyr. Shot on April 17, she was 15 and took care of her sister and six brothers while her mother worked full time in the kitchen at Caritas Hospital in Bethlehem. Her father has been unable to work because of health problems. On the way home from Nasser's burial, she was shot in the back of the head with a high-velocity bullet.

Youths with her saw a small group of soldiers behind them about 100 meters. One of them saw two soldiers getting ready to shoot and heard three shots. The same young man carried Rufeida's body to his house in the camp so that his sister, a nurse, could do something. She was already dead. Central District Commander [Amram] Mitzna maintains there were no soldiers in the area at the time of her killing.[2]

In July 1989 Israeli army sources claimed that Rufeida was killed "by local Arabs who tried to attack and kill IDF [Israel Defence Force] soldiers and who missed their target."[3] In March 1990 Israel's minister of defense, Moshe Arens, supplied the following details in response to questions raised nine months earlier by Knesset member Yair Tsaban:

On April 17, 1989, a curfew was imposed on Deheishe. An IDF patrol spotted a disturbance and the soldiers acted to disperse it. At a certain stage the supply of rubber bullets ran out and the soldiers' lives were threatened by the throwing of stones and bottles. One of the commanders fired two plastic bullets, but his firing deviated from the relevant operational orders. Apparently one of these bullets hit the deceased and caused her death. As more than three months have elapsed since the sergeant's demobilization, he cannot be placed on disciplinary trial, and given that the circumstances of the shooting were in his favor (the feeling that his and his soldiers' lives were endangered) and that the rubber bullets had run out, the [district military prosecutor] directed the battalion commander to censure the sergeant severely for deviating from orders. It bears stressing that the military prosecutor took this step despite the life-threatening situation in which the unit found itself.[4]

According to Arens's report, Rufeida was a victim of a bullet that "deviated from the relevant operational orders." But in a report the following month, photographs of Rufeida's exit wound, according to an Israeli human rights publication, "suggest that the bullet had been fired from extremely close range."[5] A plastic bullet fired from any distance would not have had the same results. In fact, only the use of a high-velocity bullet that explodes into fragments on impact can account for such devastation. It was the same kind of bullet that had exploded throughout Mohammad's lower abdomen nearly a year before.

The youth who carried Rufeida to his house was Ziad, the son of the man who told me the founding story of Deheishe. Ziad's sister was the nurse who tried to help. At my prodding, Ziad gave me a fuller description of the demonstrations that so often take place in Deheishe on news of a martyr's death.

Within an hour of news about a martyr's death, Deheishe youths would begin gathering outside his or her home. The gathering would turn into a funeral procession if friends were successful in kidnapping the body from the hospital and bringing it by back roads to the family. If not, the body would customarily be taken away by soldiers for autopsy at the Abu Kbir Institute near Tel Aviv. Burial would then wait for days, sometimes weeks, for its return to the family, who would have to undergo the further ignominy of arranging to collect the body at Bethlehem civil administration offices. Religious edict on martyrdom calls for the body's immediate burial in the state the person was left, with no washing or changing of clothes. Bodies taken for autopsy, however, are returned with incisions from neck to pubic bone, even when the victim has died from a head injury. For a time, unconfirmed rumor had it that organs were being harvested from the bodies before release, particularly from Gazan victims of head injury who were taken by army helicopter to an Israeli hospital in Tel Aviv.

Alerted to the death, soldiers would converge on the same neighborhood as the gathering youths. While the two groups were readying themselves for confrontation, the camp's older men like Naim and Ziad's father sometimes tried to cool the situation. They appealed to the officer to pull back his men, pointing out that the demonstration would remain peaceful if only the army would stay at a distance. By this time, the officer had already ordered the youths to return to their own homes. Neither side willing to back down, the drama of stones and bullets would inevitably unfold. By the spring of 1989, these demonstrations had taken on a predictable pattern that helps to explain the clustering of deaths like those of Imad, Nasser, and Rufeida.

It was during such a drama that Nasser was shot as he was picking up a stone to throw at the soldiers who were already expecting a reaction to the death of Imad. Rufeida must have thought she had escaped this pattern as she was returning home from Nasser's burial the following day. The friends of Nasser and Rufeida say that the pattern will continue until they have their legitimate rights in a state of their own.

Mohammad was the ninth Intifada martyr in Deheishe Camp. Twelve-year-old Bassem al-Ghrouz became the camp's tenth martyr the next February. I was told the story of his death during my post-Gulf War return to Deheishe by one of the *shabab* who happened to witness it from a friend's balcony. Bassem was shot by a soldier who was part of a clash in Irtas, the neighboring village where Mohammad, Nasser, and Rufeida had been buried. Bassem watched the clash from the mountainside above the camp where he had been shepherding the family's several sheep and goats. Taken up in the excitement of the distant melee, he had thrown a stone that landed far short of the soldier. Noting the boy in the distance, the soldier took aim and shot him anyway.

On hearing the shot and seeing the boy fall, the witness ran to the site, picked up Bassem, and rushed him in his Volkswagen Beetle to a Bethlehem hospital where he was dead on arrival. When the witness returned Bassem's body to his religious family in Deheishe, they declared that their son would live forever as a martyr. It was the soldier, they said, who had died. Bassem was buried in the crypt right next to Mohammad. To its right, the small cemetery of Deheishe martyrs looks across to the convent and monastery side of the mountain where 1,432 dunams of land, about 360 acres, were confiscated—for the expansion of a nearby Jewish settlement—on the occasion of U.S. Secretary of State James Baker's visit on April 24, 1991, some six months before the opening of Middle East peace talks in Madrid. Thus far, Solomon's gardens continue to remain within sight of the Deheishe graves.

Chapter 6

Second Return: After the Gulf War

"They don't put as much value on life over there": How many times did I hear these words from U.S. citizens during the Iran-Iraq war, when, on the nightly news, we could view the kamikaze-like behavior of Arab masses filling up our television screens. Hundreds would rush forward on the battlefield, shouting "Allahu akbar!" (God is great!), and then fall, scores at a time, instant martyrs in what they considered a holy war (jihad).

Then again in the Gulf War, when upwards of 100,000 Iraqis were killed somewhere beyond the reach of the networks, we could find ways of condoning the megatons of reportedly precision bombing—a "painless Nintendo exercise," as Palestinian-American scholar Edward Said described it. After all, we could say, Muslims were always ready to die for their assured place in paradise.

What continued to impress me in Deheishe Refugee Camp was not how much people were willing to die but how much they wanted to live. It seems no longer ago than yesterday that Mohammad's parents and I were talking about how we had to find a way of keeping him alive. Late into the night, we talked about what had to be done between then, a cold winter night more than six years ago, and the time he could have a small-bowel transplant. Mohammad was willing to take the risk immediately, but his Boston doctor wanted to buy time until the procedure had been tested on more human subjects—or at least until Mohammad had no other options. He had been doing well on hyperalimentation except for the infections that are expected in the kind of long-term nutritional infusion that requires daily (or nightly, in Mohammad's case) hooking up of a tube to a permanent chest catheter whose site must be kept sterile.

We sat in the salon that night, the room cooking hot with two heaters, a kerosene stove and the electric *soba* I had huddled next to the last time I had slept in the camp. We talked about how we could not allow ourselves to be overwhelmed. One thing at a time, we agreed. It would take longer than thirteen days this time around, maybe years. First, there was the outstanding bill for those initial months at Deaconess Hospital. It had to be paid to keep their doors open to Mohammad in case of an emergency that could not be handled at Makassad. Second, physical therapy had to be arranged to strengthen Mohammad's abdominal muscles, weakened by so many incisions, in preparation for the transplant. Third, there was the transplant itself, which Mohammad was so eager to have. Was he really aware of the risks? Did he imagine that a transplant would solve all his problems rather than exchange them for the new and maybe bigger problem of possible organ rejection? No one seemed to know what was in Mohammad's mind except for an unflinching resolve to go ahead with the procedure as soon as possible.

Those were the big problems ahead. In the meantime, there were the day-to-day problems: calling on the United Nations (UNRWA) to deliver his food supply when the camp was under curfew, fighting the stubbornness that kept Mohammad from going to Makassad when his temperature spiked, the same "noncompliance" that must have helped keep him alive in those early weeks when everyone except his mother was waiting for him to die. And then there was the letter we wanted to get from the West Bank military commander that would keep soldiers from detaining him, a constant worry of his mother and father.

I wanted to get an audience with Captain Kamel, the Druze assistant to the Bethlehem military governor, to facilitate the laissez-passer that Mohammad would be needing for his second trip to Boston. When and with what money, we did not yet know. What we did know was that, in Nidal's special form of English, Mohammad "must to live."

Some months later, I had that audience with the captain. Many of the Druze, a religious group with secretly held beliefs, lived in the Golan Heights, which Israel had annexed from Syria after the 1967 war. The only non-Jews required to serve in the Israeli military, some of them were notorious for their cruel behavior, both in the regular army and especially in the longer-serving border police who operated in East Jerusalem and certain parts of the Gaza Strip. It was the border police who opened unprovoked fire on Palestinians at Al-Aksa Mosque in the late summer of 1990, killing 17 and injuring 136. It was also the border police who killed five and injured upwards of eighty-five in the Nahalin massacre in April 1989.

Captain Kamel received me in the traditional manner of a village *mukhtar*. He first thanked me for giving him the privilege of hearing my request and then scolded Naim, who had accompanied me, for not coming to him sooner to ask for his help. The captain's Arabic was translated for me by a man in civilian clothes who sat next to him and directly across from me. Naim later identified him as a member of the Shin Bet, the Israeli secret security service. Kamel was in full uniform and, with high cheekbones, warm brown skin, and icy-blue eyes, he looked like a Bedouin chieftain out of David Lean's *Lawrence of Arabia*. As soon as I identified the purpose of my call, the captain signed a slip of paper to take to the office responsible for putting the laissez-passer request in motion. Travel permission was granted in less than a week, and Mohammad and I were soon off to Boston with promises of funding that never arrived. Those broken promises would contribute to his death a year later when the doors of Deaconess Hospital closed once again to further tests and treatment. An Israeli army officer, however, had come through for us. That his motive—to dispense a favor that reinforced his power and our dependence—was far from serving any Palestinian sense of justice made no difference. Mohammad's life was being saved.

Some two years later, I found other life-enhancing activity in full force when, at the end of my school year in the States, I returned to Deheishe for a post-Gulf War visit. I had expected to find demoralization in the camp; like the rest of the West Bank, it had been under curfew for the duration of the Gulf War, from January 15 until February 28. In fact, the Deheishe curfew began eleven days earlier when on January 4 a protesting group of Jewish settlers had prevented the visiting U.N. General Assembly president, then an Italian, from entering and touring the camp. On February 17, Deheishe residents sent a formal letter of protest to the U.N. secretary general. The curfew was then in its forty-fourth day and the economic situation in the camp was "on the verge of collapsing," they warned. No one had been allowed to leave the camp for work, and residents had been given a total of only six hours in the first forty-two days of the curfew to renew fast-dwindling supplies of canned goods. Fresh fruit and vegetables had long since disappeared from the mom-and-pop-style camp markets. By the end, people were down to rice and lentils.

Not only had Deheishe residents lost weight and income during the Gulf War. Having supported Saddam Hussein, they, along with the rest of the Palestinian population on the West Bank and Gaza, had lost the moral high ground that three years of their uprising had gained for them in the eyes of most of the world. They were the war's big losers, and Israel, the unretaliating victim of Iraqi Scuds, was its big winner.

Since the war, Jewish settlement activity had accelerated under housing minister Ariel Sharon, and, by mid-April 1991, Israel had succeeded in taking control of nearly two-thirds (65.5%) of the West Bank, excluding East Jerusalem, according to the Israeli newspaper *Ha'aretz* (April 17, 1991). Hundreds of thousands of Soviet and Ethiopian Jews were still on their way to the Promised Land. According to Sharon's projections, tens of thousands more units would be built on the West Bank to house them.

But instead of the long faces I expected to find, I was met everywhere in Deheishe with signs of new life. Ghada and 'Atta had moved into the large house they had begun building before I left Deheishe for the States the previous summer; white-framed windows were installed, tile was laid, and they were buying new furniture as they could afford it. Nidal was taking truck-driving lessons in the hopes of employment with UNRWA. Ziad was registered for classes at Bethlehem University and had his eye on a pretty girl from Beit Jala. Hussein and I could finally talk with one another, his having enrolled as an English major in a teachers college in Ramallah. Maysoun—the first female Intifada casualty in Deheishe, who had preceded Mohammad to the United States for medical treatment—and her fiancé had ordered the rings they would be exchanging for their engagement, wearing them on their right ring fingers until they had fixed up the small house they had bought in the camp and could get married; and then they would shift the rings to their left hands. In addition to that engagement, there were five others among the *shabab* and *benat* I knew. The seventh and eighth were also on their way: Nidal and Rafat would be announcing their respective engagements as soon as the first anniversary of Mohammad's death had passed. "We must to live," they said.

Engagements and weddings had been the big occasions for campwide celebrations before the uprising. For weddings, camp residents would fill the pathways, men carrying the groom aloft, singing national songs, and chanting factional slogans. Stringed instruments and drums would accompany the *debkah*, the Palestinian folk dance, which young men would perform into the evening. The heavily madeup bride would be dressed in a Western-style white gown against which gold necklaces, bracelets, and earrings—purchased by the groom and his family—would be shown off. Engagement celebrations, though less exuberant, would involve, at the least, a filmy new dress for the fiancée and a stylish suit for her intended. Family and friends would gather in the family home of the woman to be served refreshments and to receive commemorative tea glasses.

By decree from the Intifada leadership, no such celebrations were to take place during the uprising. Only as many people as could fit into the groom's car and the local sheik were in evidence for Intifada weddings. Music, singing, dancing, and special refreshments were put away for the day of liberation.

That was the case, at least, until Nasser's wedding, which took place only a matter of weeks after the war had ended. Since it happened before I returned for my postwar visit, I saw only the photographs of the stylish occasion that Nasser and his bride decided to create. Released with Akram from five years of imprisonment some six months before, Nasser was dressed in a double-breasted white suit, black shirt, and red tie— three of the four colors of the Palestinian flag. Only the flag's green was not in full view, but it was sure to be somewhere, perhaps in a garter beneath the satin folds of the bridal gown. Nasser told me that song and dance had also been part of the day's events, along with good food. Having earned his political stripes, Nasser had no apologies to make for the lavish, pre-Intifada-style celebration. "After all," he told me, "we have to go on living."

On approaching the Abu Aker compound when I arrived in Deheishe, I noted the new parrot-green paint on the outside gate and, on walking into the garden, I was greeted with the bright paint everywhere: on the iron poles holding up the expanded grape arbor, on the large drums of the family's backup water supply, on the stair railings up to the front-door balcony, and on the double front door as well. It was not long after my arrival that I was caught up with everyone else in preparations for a big feast for which Hala would be newly outfitted and a lamb would be slaughtered. (Given what a brat Hala could be, I sometimes thought it should be the other way around.) The family and their friends were still celebrating when I left the camp for the United States. The only long face was Hala's. She was still smarting from the punishment her mother had meted out for cutting up an antique lace shawl. Hala thought it would make just the right headband to complete her holiday outfit.

"We must live!": this had been Nidal's refrain almost from the beginning. I met him for the first time in Mohammad's hospital room at Makassad in early October 1988, two days before Mohammad would be flying to Boston. Nidal had just been released from six months of detention in Ansar III. Over the past three years, he and his twin brother, Rafat, had been in one prison or another a total of seventeen months, but never at the same time. One of them would be going in as the other was coming out. Like their younger brother, the twins were very active in the uprising.

Nidal had learned of Mohammad's injury when he was in Ansar despite the fact that fellow detainees had hidden from him the newspaper accounts about the extent of his brother's injury. Everyone had been waiting for Nidal's release. Mohammad may have hung onto life as long as he did just to be able to see Nidal again. That thought struck me when it became obvious how the rest of the family depended on his strength. I was in the hospital corridor when Naim and his oldest son greeted each other for the first time after Nidal's release. Naim had been sleeping overnight at Makassad the evening Nidal reached Deheishe. Their embrace is something I will always remember. It was only on returning from Boston to Deheishe three months later that I began to know something of the strength of character that Naim needed so desperately to enfold that morning.

It had been Nidal who, at the age of fifteen, put his foot down when his parents were considering building a new house on a plot of land across the road from Deheishe and outside the fence that had begun to define the camp's boundary. "We were forced to move from our village," he had said. "We will not move again until we return to our land." He told his parents that they had to build a good house in the camp, as good as the one his father was thinking of building on the mountain. With their own savings and help from family members then working in the Gulf states, they finished the house in 1986, when Nidal was nineteen. On the day they moved in, Mohammad was arrested for the first time and kept for eighteen days of interrogation at al-Fara'a prison, where young boys from Deheishe were regularly tortured, a few of them into collaboration. Mohammad was fifteen at the time.

Built on top of the "temporary" shelter provided by UNRWA in the mid-fifties, the substantial three-bedroom house signaled to their neighbors and the occupation authorities the Abu Akers' intention to stay put. Nothing less than the army's dynamite would move them, and then, like hundreds of other families whose houses had been demolished under military government orders, it would be only as far as the tent they would set up in the middle of the rubble.

Two years earlier, Nidal had been chosen to speak for a Deheishe group that organized a protest against the reduced food allowance that UNRWA had been distributing during the Israeli invasion of Lebanon. Deheishe's allotment, like the allotments going to all refugees in the Occupied Territories, had been cut back to meet the increased need of Palestinian camps under Israeli bombardment to the north. Palestinians on the West Bank and in Gaza should not have to pay for Israel's war, he told UNRWA officials in East Jerusalem.

When Nidal and I began our talks, his English was halting. He insisted, however, on speaking it as often as he could. He wanted to be able to tell Mohammad's story to the foreigners who bought gas at the Bethlehem station where he worked with his father and to the steady stream of Western journalists who visited Deheishe Camp during the first two years of the uprising. In the telling and retelling of Mohammad's story, he showed neither anger nor bitterness, only a strong resolve.

With a patience that belied his youth—he was then in his early twenties—he would talk about the time it would take for Palestinians to reach their goal of self-determination and statehood. "Maybe my children will see it," he would say to me. For anything to happen, every Palestinian must be "touched" by the Occupation, he said, not just the people in the camps. Suffering must be experienced by the businessmen in Bethlehem and Jerusalem, not just by the people of Deheishe. They, too, must go to prison; their sons and daughters "must be shot like Mohammad." This could take a long time, but "history," he would say, "is on our side." The Marxist-Leninist dialectics that inform his and his friends' resolve have now fallen on hard times. Palestinians like Nidal may turn out to be the last holdouts in a world moving away from the left. When at those times I listened to him with my Western ear, I feared that he too would become history.

I had another kind of history lesson when I visited Nidal's high school in the late summer of 1989, a few weeks before I took Mohammad back to Boston for his followup examination. Being back in school again was itself historic, since all West Bank educational institutions had been closed for a year. As a result of mounting international pressure, Israel had opened the primary and secondary schools, although they kept the universities closed.

For Nidal and five of his Deheishe friends to be back in school was nothing less than a victory, since all of them had long since been permanently expelled from the Israeli government-run high schools from the time of their first arrests. Since Deheishe had a long history of resistance, hundreds of camp youth had been out of school because of their records of political arrest, most often without any formal charges. Unable to learn through regular channels, they managed nonetheless to continue their education in prison. "Prison," they would say, "is our Palestinian university."

Nidal and his friends were determined to pass the final high school exams (*tawjihi*) that would be given at the end of November. Unable to reenter their former high school in Bethlehem, they made arrangements on their own to register for a semester at the private school Mohammad had been attending before he was shot. It was a Latin Catholic school in Beit Sahour, a largely Christian Palestinian village near Bethlehem that was to become famous for its tax war against the Occupation.

The only Muslims in their English, Arabic, and history classes, they clearly kept the teachers on their toes. Except for English, the classes crackled with the questions, comments, and occasional corrections coming from the back row, across which the Deheishe *shabab* spread themselves. The English teacher, like many of his American counterparts, nearly managed to kill the subject with his prissiness. The Arabic teacher, in contrast, presented the subtleties of grammar and inscription with the skill and daring of a trapeze artist.

The history teacher, however, was the clear favorite of the Deheishe contingent, not so much for his brilliance as for his devotion to both his subject matter and his students. The day's lesson was on the early Ottoman Empire, but he kept breaking in with broken English, clearly for my benefit, to lament the present situation. Correcting his English and then questioning and supplementing his presentation, the Deheishe *shabab* were well aware that his earnest sentiments sometimes blurred the historical record. One of them turned to me and warned, sotto voce, "You should not believe everything this teacher says." Knowing and accepting the history teacher's limitations—"He is a simple man," Nidal had whispered that day—they nonetheless loved him. History had come alive in his classroom, not so much the history they were studying as the history they were making, the foolish along with the wise.

I learned a lot from Nidal. In a letter of recommendation I wrote for his application to Bethlehem University, I said the following:

> Over the last two years, I have come to know Nidal Abu Aker as an extraordinary young man. Because of his resistance activity and numerous detentions, he, like most of his peers in Deheishe Camp, has had difficulty completing his high school education. It was Nidal who last fall organized a group of his friends for the purpose of finishing high school and preparing for the high school diploma. He was able to arrange their several months' attendance at the private Latin Catholic school in Beit Sahour where his brother, Mohammad, studied until his injury.
>
> I'll always remember what Nidal said to me several months ago: "You must love your teacher and you must love your books." Having been a university professor for nearly twenty years, I was struck by the simple profundity of what he had to say about an education that *means* something. I have found him to have an endlessly interested and interesting mind, able not only to explain clearly the facts of a given situation but also capable of serious analysis and wise reflection.
>
> Although I have never had him as one of my students, I have had the good fortune to be in *his* classroom. He has taught me a great deal not only about Palestinian history and politics but also about life as such.

Life as such: it was much too vague and even ponderous a phrase for what I actually had in mind, but talk about promenades did not quite fit the genre of a university recommendation letter. *Promenades* was the word I used for the spring evening walks that we took through the camp after more than half a year of night curfews was finally lifted. Beginning in mid-September 1989 and lasting until April 17 of the following year, Deheishe residents had to stay inside their houses from 6:00 in the evening until 5:30 the following morning. The confinement became increasingly irksome when the cold and often rainy winter weather began to give way to the softest of springs. Being deprived of such lovely evenings was especially difficult for the young men and women who would otherwise be sauntering in their separate groups through the pathways, exchanging glances and greetings and lingering outside the little house shops that sold soda and ice cream. Like their cohorts in the free world, they wanted to celebrate the rites of spring.

The promenades began the evening the curfew was lifted, on April 17, the beginning of the feast days that followed the month of Ramadan fasting. As it turned out, the night curfew was reimposed a week later and, after another brief respite, reimposed yet again on July 18, ten days before I arrived back in the United States. So it was stolen time that we spent on the camp pathways, although we did not know it at the time.

We did know, however, that that first walk was, in effect, a ritual of reclamation. Out of bounds during the seemingly endless curfew, the promenades began with purposefulness as well as gusto. Groups of young men and women set out to traverse the entire length of the camp, from its southern boundary to its northern edge, both taking back the pathways and taking in the balmy air.

We set out that night from the Abu Aker house near the southern boundary and headed north, Mohammad Hussein, Khaled, Abdel Azziz, Ziad, Salah, Rafat, Nidal, and I. Mohammad Abu Aker could not join us, since this was the time he attached himself to the dropper machine to begin his overnight infusion.

Darkness settles all at once in that part of the world. There were no street lights in the camp, so the way was dark except for indoor lighting and lit television screens. The *shabab*, however, knew every step of the way, having run through the pathways so often in eluding the army patrols that would order them to show their identity cards and often rough them up or take them away for eighteen days of interrogation. I grabbed one arm or another to avoid turning my ankle in the sewer channels or tripping over the stones. I took turns keeping my eyes to the uneven ground and looking up to catch the stars and little points of house lights that masked the daytime ugliness of the camp.

It was when my head was down that we ran into an army patrol. When one of the soldiers shone his flashlight in our faces, Nidal and the others were prepared for the usual trouble. But most likely because I was with them, the officer nodded us on our way with a "Good evening." We stopped not long afterward near the northern boundary of the camp to buy one of the local Palestinian colas produced by the Royal Crown factory in Ramallah. A family was selling the soft drinks out of the ground-floor UNRWA room in which they had formerly lived. Like the Abu Akers, they had built new living quarters above the concrete block module that had once housed the grandparents.

All along the way, voices greeted me. Young men and women I had met at the Abu Akers or the many who had seen me coming in and going out of the camp over those past two years knew who I was, even in the dark. One of them called out, "It's just like the streets of Paris!"

"Even better," I answered. On these little pathways through a West Bank refugee camp, I felt far more at home than in Paris.

In addition to the life-affirming promenades before I left the West Bank, there was an evening of drinking beer with my young friends when I returned to Deheishe after the Gulf War. Like Southern Baptists, most Muslims frown on alcoholic beverages. But we were celebrating not just our reunion but also the fact that life was continuing to go on. "It's what we will drink every day in paradise," Nidal jokingly said in the Bethlehem restaurant that specialized in American-style hamburgers and large steins of draft beer: "big beer," they called it, *biera kbiera*. It was not, however, the Islamic paradise Nidal and his friends were rushing to enter, even though their continuing resistance activity kept them close to the possibility of death at almost every turn. Despite all the holy war mythology, martyrdom had no edge on the full lives my Palestinian friends insisted on living.

When I came back to Deheishe on the occasion of Mohammad's death, Nidal told me that Mohammad had finally joined the *shabab* on one of their promenades that spring. He had been able to fit in another piece of Deheishe's life before he died. In a final life-enhancing gesture, he insisted that his drinking water be brought in from the camp during his last hours in the intensive care unit.

My post-Gulf War visit was not only to find out how my friends were faring. I also wanted to inquire after the health of the Intifada. After a week in the camp, I visited two American friends in East Jerusalem. They gave me a bleak picture of things. "The Intifada has collapsed," one of them reported. The other told me it was "dead." Both reports disturbed me because they were so much at odds with my impression of things in Deheishe. More than that, they seemed such abstract and distant pronouncements.

To be sure, the problems were greater than ever. Continuing to have an impact on the present situation were the prewar massacres: first, on "Bloody Sunday" when a soldier had gunned down seven Gazan day laborers who were waiting at a pickup area for possible day work; then at Al-Aksa Mosque in October when seventeen Palestinians had been victims of unprovoked shooting by the Jerusalem border police. Added to those shocking events was the postwar crisis for thousands of Palestinians who had been working in Kuwait and were now being imprisoned, tortured, and executed for alleged support of Iraq. There was concern not only about what that ongoing crisis meant for their relatives' personal safety but also about what the political upheaval meant for the economy of the West Bank and Gaza, which had long counted on remittances sent back home by those relatives working in the Gulf.

Out on the Abu Akers' roof, I spent an evening getting an analysis of the difficult situation from Hamdi Faraj, a Deheishe neighbor and well-known journalist who ran a press office in Bethlehem. Hamdi had solid credentials: he had been in prison seventeen times, had spent a total of three and a half years under house arrest, and had had his magazine and then his newspaper closed by the Israeli government in 1983 and in 1986. His brother, Jamal, was deported to Lebanon at the beginning of 1989 on charges of directing the uprising.

Hamdi had recently written an article about the state of the Intifada, and he outlined his ideas for me over the tea, coffee, cola, and fruit that Malka continued to serve us as we sat on the mats that had been shifted to the roof from the traditional salon.

"The Intifada is, first of all, a movement of the people," Hamdi pointed out, "not a program run by seasoned diplomats. The movement runs deep, and it has made mistakes."

One of the biggest mistakes, he suggested, had been paying too little attention to unaffiliated people, the ones who had gone unrepresented by the Palestinian party structure and were therefore more vulnerable to Israeli economic, military, and psychological pressures.

"These are the people who are growing impatient and who are losing hope," Hamdi said. "Their problems *must* be taken into account in future planning by the leadership."

When I mentioned the bleak reports from my friends in East Jerusalem, Hamdi said, "Too much has been deposited into the Intifada account to close it now." He was talking about the martyrdoms and the injuries that had permanently disabled a generation of young men (and some young women like Maysoun) as well as the unmeasurable traumas that had been suffered by hundreds of young children who had witnessed the beating of their fathers and older brothers, and even their mothers and sisters, by soldiers invading their homes. To illustrate how the "account" was being kept open, Hamdi told me about a recent demonstration in the nearby "liberated" village of Batir to mark the anniversary of a martyrdom that had taken place in the first year of the Intifada:

"The demonstration went on for twenty-four hours," Hamdi said, "and the villagers carried more than a hundred outlawed Palestinian flags." Defense Minister Arens had been trying to kill the Intifada through neglect rather than through his predecessor Yitzhak Rabin's policy of breaking Palestinian bones. Through orders to avoid confrontation with Palestinian demonstrators, Arens hoped to starve the Intifada of media coverage and thereby to kill it: out of sight, out of mind.

"But the mothers won't forget," Hamdi said.

I thought of the mothers who had made their rounds in the camp that past week after getting news of Ya'coub's arrest. At such news, the women would put on their long embroidered dresses and make their way through the camp to call on the mothers of youths who had been taken away by soldiers, to hear their reports and to show their solidarity with them. I went with Malka and her neighbor, Um Taysir, to call on Ya'coub's mother the morning after he was taken away by soldiers. We also paid a call on the mother of a twelve-year-old across the pathway on the late afternoon I myself had seen five soldiers chase him with their M-16s pointed at him after he had tossed a stone in their direction. His grandmother, Um Azziz, had come out to rescue him after he had been cornered. His mother told us he had wet his pants in fear.

Hamdi was long overdue for chemotherapy in London, where he had been going since being diagnosed in January 1988 with Hodgkin's disease. He was waiting, he told me, until his current identity card expired. He, like thousands on the West Bank, had been issued a green card in early December forbidding travel into Israel. A form of collective punishment, the cards were a response to the random stabbings of Israelis that followed the Al-Aksa massacre.

Most of the Deheishe green cards had been issued between nine in the evening and four the next morning on December 4 and 5. Military patrols carrying computerized printouts entered all homes that listed male occupants between sixteen and thirty-five. Additional cards were issued at a checkpoint set up the following day at the camp's main entrance. Scores of camp residents had lost their jobs in Israel as a result of the travel restriction or because they had been replaced by newly immigrated Soviet Jews. Hamdi hoped that he would soon be getting a red card that would allow him to travel to Ben-Gurion Airport, where he could catch a plane to London. When he left the Abu Akers' that night, I was sure he had other things on his mind, not the state of his own health.

What Nidal and his friends had on their minds was the prospect of an American solution imposed on the region. "The people of Deheishe refuse an American solution," he and others said with a nervous chuckle, fearing they would have little choice in the matter. After the massive American victory in the Gulf War, such an imposition seemed unavoidable. They viewed the recent appointment of the new Jordanian prime minister, a personal friend of King Hussein as well as a friend of U.S. interests in the region, as a first step in that direction. That the new prime minister was also close to Yasser Arafat was especially troubling, since they regarded Arafat as a leader they could not trust to stand up against the United States. What had long been known as the Jordanian Solution, favored by Israel's Labor and Likud Parties as well as by the United States, seemed to be moving out of the wings onto center stage. It could mean a confederation between Jordan's East Bank and part of the West Bank or, in the Likud version, a transfer of West Bank Palestinians to Jordan. In neither case would there be a Palestinian state.

With all that, Nidal and his friends continued to draw the same bottom line: "Nothing that the Palestinians do not agree to will succeed; the stone throwing will not stop; the Intifada will continue." Another of the Deheishe youths I met at the Bethlehem University cafeteria opened things up a bit more: "Things are now unclear," he said. "We need time to think about where we are and where we need to go. Peace is now more complicated." No talk anywhere, however, of the Intifada's collapse or death.

The most telling report on the Intifada came out of a set of responses I was given when, asked about when I was coming back to Deheishe again, I said, "Next year." Two people—a sixty-five-year-old woman and twelve-year-old Joffer—responded to my answer with the same words: "Maybe I'll be dead by then." This response told me more about the continuous life of the Intifada than any political analysis I had heard. Resistance had become a law of nature in Deheishe. Cutting across genders and generations, revolution had become a habit of thought, feeling, and action. That it was a matter for debate down the road in East Jerusalem struck me as irrelevant.

The story of Deheishe during the Gulf War I learned in bits and pieces. Most of what I heard was anecdotal. For instance, a neighbor had happened to be awake when the war started about 2:00 a.m. his time. Unable to get back to sleep after the Shin Bet had come to his home to pick up his brother-in-law about 11:30 p.m., he heard camp sirens and shouts to turn on the radio some two and a half hours later. He kept four radios and two television sets going for the next forty-eight days.

Several people told me that camp residents had thrown their radios out the window that night. Until the next day, they had been able to get only reports that indicated early and complete defeat of Saddam Hussein. Along with most West Bankers, Deheishe residents backed Saddam—not his occupation of Kuwait but his willingness to stand up against the United States, whose foreign aid had financed the Israeli Occupation for more than twenty years.

When the Scuds began to land in Tel Aviv, the camp took on a carnival atmosphere. Cooped up under weeks of curfew, Deheishe residents could at last come outside to join with friends and neighbors as the soldiers, hastily donning the gas masks that had been attached to their legs, ran out of the camp to the military station across the road. It would be the soldiers who were cooped up inside plastic-lined shelters while the camp residents were outside watching the light show from their rooftops. One neighbor told me he had shouted to the soldiers twice as the Scuds were flying and they were running out of Deheishe. Once he informed them that the missiles were not chemical, a good thing since gas masks had not been distributed to camp residents other than UNRWA employees; another time he had shouted, as if he were a taxi driver, "Ten shekels from Baghdad to Tel Aviv!" The neighbor's second daughter was born on the last day of the war. He and his wife named her Salaam, the Arabic word for peace.

Nidal added several other details about life in the camp during the war. There had been more cats in the garden, he said. Instead of the usual family of six, there had been closer to twenty of those long, triangular-headed felines one sees all over the streets of the West Bank. Hunger had driven them inside the walled compound. He also told me about being for a brief time in a small room at Bethlehem military headquarters with a retarded camp resident, Jibril, whom I remember clearly from Mohammad's homecoming celebration in March 1989. Jibril had heartily shaken Rafat's hand instead of Mohammad's and we—including Jibril—had all laughed. While Nidal had been sharing his cell with Jibril, a Scud had flown overhead and Jibril had shouted "Sadaam, Sadaam!" at the top of his lungs. Nidal had been a bit nervous about what might happen to the pair of them.

More seriously, Nidal talked about Iraq as the one Arab state that had been moving beyond what he called an "occupation mentality." He was referring to the occupation under which the Middle East had been living since the division of the area between France and Britain in the secret

Sykes-Picot agreement just after World War I. Before that, it had been under Turkish occupation for four hundred years during the Ottoman Empire. When Nidal described present-day Iraq's move beyond occupation mentality, he was referring to the country's developing means of production, including the production of nuclear capability, that would free Iraq from dependence on Europe and the United States. It was the move toward economic independence more than Iraq's invasion of Kuwait, he said, that triggered U.S. intervention.

One of the *shabab* later added to the Gulf War analysis when two Swiss journalists were visiting the Abu Akers. The United States needed to protect and enhance its international interests in light of economic advances being made by Japan and the European Community, he said. "The whole of the Middle East is now under American occupation," he concluded.

For Hamdi, the worst part of the war was living in isolation from friends and neighbors because of the curfew, though it was repeatedly broken—in fact, on the first morning of the war, when residents staged a large demonstration at 6:00 a.m. Deheishe needed more than ever to express its solidarity. Without gas masks, the camp was more vulnerable than the Israelis in the event of chemical attack, a danger that the widely reported dancing on rooftops did nothing to diminish.

School exams ended the morning of June 18, and a demonstration began within minutes. Once again we had front-row seats in the Abu Akers' veranda. At the bottom of the road, boys and girls were hurling stones over the high zinc-paneled fence at the military station across the road. The demonstration seemed at first like a children's game of cops and robbers, but the soldiers soon began using live ammunition.

It was in such a demonstration that Lutfi was shot in the head last year. He had been in a semiconscious state in Makassad Hospital when I came back for Mohammad's death. Now he was back in the camp after a first regimen of physical therapy at the new center of the Bethlehem Arab Society for Rehabilitation in Beit Jala. He walked about the camp with a cane, his right hand strapped into a plastic mold to keep his paralyzed fingers from retracting. There was always a friend with him, usually Iman, on whose shoulder he could lean whenever he wanted. At that time, he was wearing a trucker's cap to cover his head, which had been shaved for the latest surgery to repair the crater made by the bullet. He would need more therapy before his doctor could determine if his memory loss and aphasia were permanent. Meanwhile, he smiled a lot.

When Hala got home from school, she reported that she and her class-mates began to sing at news of the stone throwing and then to dance when, in short order, a curfew was announced. The UNRWA teachers dismissed the children classroom by classroom so that they could get to their homes in small groups. On her way up the hill, Hala reported, some soldiers were beating a boy.

Nidal turned up the volume on the radio to catch news of the demon-stration that would probably be announced soon on Al-Quds Radio, a station broadcasting from outside Israel and the Occupied Territories. Its facilities had been destroyed by the Israelis earlier in the Intifada. Nidal thought that their being back on the air was part of the negotiations then taking place for the release of seven Israeli military prisoners being held in South Lebanon. News like the Deheishe demonstration was faxed to the station through local contacts who got it by telephone. I heard other news while we were waiting for the Deheishe report:

—Two soldiers were injured by a bomb in Nablus.

—A settler's car was burned in Ramallah.

—A Molotov cocktail was thrown in Rafah.

—Through wall writing, warnings have been issued against participat-ing in elections of West Bank committees to handle international fund-ing for economic development. The candidates were being described as collaborators.

Malka reported that Jibril (he was the one who shouted "Saddam, Saddam!" in the cell he shared with Nidal) had just been picked up for breaking the curfew. Released within hours, he would be joining us later in my visit for an evening on the roof.

Malka began another labor-intensive meal, sitting on the floor with Nida'. Both of them were hollowing out the centers of small zucchinis. They would fill the empty centers with a mixture of rice, garlic, parsley, and small bits of meat. The stuffed vegetables would be simmered in the juice pressed from tomatoes and a rich liquid reconstituted from dried chunks of yogurt.

More news on Al-Quds Radio while we waited for the announcement about Deheishe:

—A fifty-year-old man was beaten unconscious when he gave his name, Arafat, to soldiers. Doctors fear permanent brain damage. The man's son is serving a 100-year sentence in prison and his home was demolished last month. (I forgot to ask Nidal where the man was from.)

—Curfews have been clamped in Nablus and Rafah.

—A house was demolished in Silwan, a neighborhood in East Jerusalem.

News of the Deheishe demonstration came on at 12:30 p.m. They said the stone throwing that began at 9:30 that morning was continuing. The Occupation army, as Palestinians call the Israel Defence Force (IDF), responded with live ammunition and tear gas, but no casualties were reported as yet. The demonstration must have been taking place in other parts of the camp, since the only activity I saw from the veranda was "Abu Waji'" running like crazy up the road. One of Mohammad's best friends, Abu Waji' had been on the camp's wanted list for two and a half years. His oldest brother gave him the nickname, the nom de guerre of a Popular Front hijacker in the late sixties, when he was a child. Unable to sleep at home, where soldiers regularly looked for him, he had become another son of the camp, sleeping and eating wherever he happened to be. A shy fellow, he had played straight man to Mohammad's crazy antics.

Although his three brothers were Bethlehem University graduates, Abu Waji' decided to study car mechanics at the UNRWA school near Ramallah. All the *shabab* had him check out their used cars before buying them. He passed inspection on Mohammad's white Fiat, which Rafat now drives. He had to stop going to school when he was issued a green card last December. Going to the West Bank city of Ramallah required passing through East Jerusalem, which was forbidden territory to green card holders, even for Friday prayers at Al-Aksa Mosque.

Later in the day, Salah slipped over from his house across the path. He and I had one of those long "curfew talks" that started out with my telling him that my American students had a low opinion of the Middle East because of its treatment of women. He began by blaming Islam and ended by singing the praises of Western technological culture. I found myself taking sides against technology and trying my best to interpret Islam in a better light. At least we managed to fill some of the time that hangs so heavy during curfews.

(While Malka was getting some bread dough ready to rise overnight, Naim nodded in her direction and said to me, finger circling at his temple, "majnouna"—crazy. I knew what he was actually saying: "I love that woman.")

The two days of curfew had been well timed to do the heavy cleaning for Id al-Adha, the feast that commemorates the slaughter of the lamb by the patriarch Abraham, who had initially been ordered by God to sacrifice his son. For Muslims, it was Ishmael, not Isaac, who was to be sacrificed. Ishmael, Abraham's son by his servant Hagar, was his firstborn, and from him Muslims trace their origin. The three-day feast is one of the most important times in the Muslim year. Nidal and Rafat removed furniture and mats to scrub all the floors; Naim and Nida' took out the sliding windows in the veranda to hose them down and dry them with newspapers. Everyone took part in the big cleaning, even the young women and children who dropped by. Since they were less likely to be arrested or shot, they were the message carriers during curfews.

On the second day of the curfew, Hanan, a neighbor, came over in the morning to make a special cake for the feast. Farina, coconut, eggs, olive oil, and yogurt—all the ingredients she mixed with her hand and then spread in a large round pan that went into the electric oven Malka uses for baking her rounds of flat bread. While the cake was still hot, Hanan forked holes in it, poured melted sugar over the top, and sprinkled it with more coconut.

In the afternoon, Malka shouted across the road to invite Um Azziz, a woman in her late eighties, to come over for tea. She is from the same village, Ras Abu Ammar, as Malka and Naim. Like most of the other Palestinian exiles, she had been willing to move "temporarily" to Deheishe in 1948, since the camp was close enough to Ras Abu Ammar to return to it quickly when the Arab armies came to defeat the Zionists. The armies never arrived. Um Azziz shares her three-room cement-block house with her daughter and four grandchildren. She usually has the front of her everyday Palestinian *thobe* tucked up into her belt while she waters the tomato plants in her slip of a garden and takes her trash out to the dump along a nearby road.

As soon as she settled herself against one of the walls in the Abu Akers' traditional salon, I asked Um Azziz about the dream she had had of Mohammad some months ago. Malka had told me about the dream, but I wanted to hear how Um Azziz herself would report it. In the dream, she had found herself in a garden of fruit trees whose branches were laden with apples and peaches and pears. Mohammad was standing in the garden with a beautiful young woman who had been waiting a long time for him to join her. Mohammad invited Um Azziz to pick the fruit, she said, but she could not reach it. He then told her that he was angry with his mother for wearing black. He wanted her to wear colorful dresses and to keep her sense of humor.

Um Azziz's inability to reach the branches and the reference to Malka's humor were entirely believable. Um Azziz stands barely four feet tall and with her bowed legs looks even shorter. Malka can rarely be found without a broad grin unless, straight-faced, she is plying her talent at mimicry, which comes right out of comic melodrama on Egyptian television. The garden setting of the dream obviously conforms to popular versions of the Islamic as well as the Jewish and Christian images of paradise with its figures of Adam and Eve. A reminder of Solomon's gardens just below Mohammad's crypt in Irtas, the dream's setting also conformed to memories of the orchards that Palestinians like Um Azziz and Abu Ziad had left behind when they fled Ras Abu Ammar and Zakariya. How very sweet, I thought to myself, that Mohammad has a beautiful girl at his side in this old woman's dream! He would have liked that and so, obviously, would Malka. Both women welcomed the dream as a clear and comforting sign of Mohammad's well-being.

We were prepared for another day of indoor activity since, under the new rules, stone throwing automatically meant a three-day curfew. To our surprise, the curfew was lifted the following morning. That meant we could shop for the new shoes that would complete Hala's feast-day outfit. Rejecting the ones that might have held together and not shown the dirt of unpaved camp roads, Hala insisted on a pair of thin-soled white pumps. Shortly after we returned from Bethlehem, an eighty-pound lamb was delivered. The animal was tied up in the garden until Abu Akram came over to slaughter and dress it just outside the gate. The father of the wanted youth Abu Waji', Abu Akram is one of several men in the camp who perform this ritual activity on the occasion of weddings, homecomings, and feasts. Once the blood was let, the skin stripped, the insides gutted, and the pieces cut and washed, the lamb would be ready to be put on the boil.

We were all set for the feast: the house was clean, Hala had her new shoes, and the cake (already half eaten) was ready for tomorrow's visitors. That evening we sat out on the roof adjoining the balcony, bringing out mats and pillows and, after little cups of Arabic coffee, enjoying the lamb's liver, which Malka sauteed in olive oil with garlic and parsley. We were joined by Jibril, free from detention and dressed to the nines in a sport coat and designer tie (Pierre Cardin), donations from a Bethlehem charity. Only among the Bethlehem and Jerusalem businessmen would one find such formal dress. Naim had replaced burned-out lightbulbs in two of the four outdoor lights, and we were illuminated brightly in the darkness that had fallen on the camp. I commented on the fact that we seemed to be the only ones having a good time in the June evening. "You are our protection," Nidal said to me.

Only minutes later, a military patrol entered the garden below. Two of the soldiers came up the steps onto the balcony and took identity cards from the men. They then went into the house accompanied by Naim and Malka. After a minute or two, I went inside to ask what the problem was. As in other home invasions when I happened to be on the scene, I asked the question in American English, the only weapon I had at my disposal. One of the soldiers responded in an unfriendly voice with his own question, also in English: "What are you doing here?" After I told him I was a friend of the family from the United States, the other soldier asked if I worked for UNRWA. I told him I was a professor of philosophy, always easier than trying to explain what religious studies was about. The second soldier, eager to "normalize" the situation, mentioned some name, presumably the name of a philosopher, and asked if I had ever read him. I asked my own question instead of answering his:

"Why have you come into the house? We were sitting outside in full view. Obviously, we have nothing to hide. We were eating and just having a good time.

"I am shocked by your coming into the house this way," I kept on. "My friends may not be shocked because it happens this way so often. For me, though, it is shocking."

The patrol left shortly after that. On their way down the stairs, the second soldier told us to have a good time. I heard him repeat the philosopher's name as they were going out the gate. "I really like his writing," he called back. It took another ten minutes for me to calm down. What astonished me the most was not the army's invasion. I was almost a veteran by then, after several other searches while I was on the scene. It was the force of my own reaction that took me by surprise.

The first morning of the feast, we went back to Irtas for the fourth time in those three weeks—this time for a more official visit that included many other people who began arriving by seven o'clock to visit the martyrs' crypts. Young boys from the camp stood at the gate to distribute sweets as the visitors left. Before the Intifada, it would have been only bitter coffee that was served. After the gathering had made its way past the five Deheishe martyrs—Nasser, Rufeida, Nabil, Mohammad, and Bassem—we went to Bethlehem to pay our respects to Mohammad's grandmother, the *hajeh*, who had died not long after her grandson. Her tomb was among those of several thousand former Deheishe residents in a public cemetery near the gas station where Naim works.

Neighbors and relatives began to arrive at the house as soon as we returned. Naim's nephew was one of the visitors, recently returned from Saudi Arabia where for ten years he had been an administrator in a private hospital in Riyadh. He and his wife, like many other Palestinians who for decades had lived and worked in Kuwait, had been given a week to leave the country a month after the Gulf War ended. A large group of *shabab* came by with a box of chocolates for the family. One of them was not yet able to use his right arm, which a soldier had broken while the young man was in detention more than a year ago. He delivered a speech of gratitude to Abu Nidal as the father of a Deheishe martyr.

The young man then surprised me with a gift, a varnished and hand-decorated wooden plaque. A tree stood in front of a cluster of little block-style houses in the background, a red sun in the middle of the sky. "YOU ARE WELCOME," it said in large capital English letters at the top of the plaque. Outlined in black, the lettering was filled in with red ink. "With all of our esteem for your best work," it continued. At the bottom, the plaque read, "Deheishe Refugee People." After a meal of lamb and rice, I left for the airport wondering how I could get the plaque and myself through the increasingly strict security check without having my luggage opened and red-tagged along with that of the Palestinians, who are always prepared for such delays.

Chapter 7

Third Return: Violating and Transforming Space

When I came back to Deheishe in October 1991 for the first anniversary of Mohammad's death, I divided my time between upstairs and downstairs at the Abu Akers', much as I did during my first return. The year before, the upper-story salon had been the receiving area for women mourners while the former salon on the ground floor had been turned into the offical mourning area for the men. During my third visit, these rooms were filled with other kinds of activity. The upstairs salon had metamorphosed from mourning space into a communications room where the family and their friends closely monitored the opening of Middle East peace talks being televised from Madrid. Eyes were directed toward a color television screen, not a banner in the colors of the Palestinian flag; ears were registering words about hoped-for harmony, not resolutions about continuing the struggle. "Today, our people under occupation are holding high the olive branch of peace," the head of the Palestinian peace delegation concluded in the plenary speech being watched in the upstairs salon.

Downstairs, the former UNRWA quarters were being transformed into a new apartment for Rafat and his future wife. While Dr. Haidar Abdul-Shafi was detailing "the steps leading to 'the new Palestine' " on the upper floor, Rafat and his friends were retiling floors, painting walls, and installing a modern kitchen and bath at the ground level.

The job of laying the tile was in the experienced hands of Ahmed. Twenty-one but looking ten years older, he had learned how to lay tile during five years of construction work in Israel. Unable over the past year to renew his work permit, he had been plying his trade in the camp. Others had prepared the foundation for the tiles, breaking up the old concrete floor with jackhammers, hauling in the sand, and mixing the new cement. But it was Ahmed who painstakingly measured, leveled, and tamped down each foot-square tile, gently hammering against the edges of the border and corner pieces so that he could fit them together like jigsaw puzzle pieces against the uneven walls. When I wasn't watching the Madrid broadcast, I would pull up a little plastic-roped stool to watch Ahmed's every move.

Malka, too, divided her time between upstairs and downstairs. Beyond sitting and watching like me, she filled buckets with sand and scraped up loose wet cement. She also added to her regular household chores an almost-hourly delivery of tea and coffee to the workers as well as to the neighbors, young and old, who were dropping in to watch and sometimes give advice. Like other nonlethal activity in the camp, the occasion had been turned into a neighborhood party, complete with cassette tapes of Um Kalthum's love songs and Marcel Khalifeh's national ballads.

Metamorphoses were under way outdoors as well as inside the house. In addition to helping rehabilitate the interior of the old quarters, Naim took it upon himself to beautify the area just outside the door that opened onto the road leading down to the camp fence. The road's lower exit having long been sealed off by a line of large barrels filled with concrete, the road was now used as a turnaround for residents' vehicles and for UNRWA's delivery of emergency water or for its tank-truck suctioning of solid waste from septic systems. Except for soldiers who stationed themselves at its two main intersections or leaned against the compound walls that lined it on either side, no one lingered along this road whose dirt and litter made people want to pass through as quickly as possible.

In the small area next to the compound wall and immediately next to the ugly road, Naim decided to build a small entry patio. Squares of tile set into a grid of cement mixed with small colored stones produced a striking mosaic floor when it was polished with an electric sander. Along the road side of the completed floor, Naim then built a three-foot-high stuccoed wall, which he topped with slabs of pink marble that picked up the color of the embedded stones. The patio stopped short of transforming the entire road, but a six- by ten-foot section adjoining that road was successfully rescued for less profane use—"unless," as I joked with Naim, "the soldiers confiscate the patio for an outdoor café." I suggested they could stop off for an Arabic coffee break during their twenty-four-hour patrolling of the camp.

In fact, passing soldiers took great interest in the whole downstairs enterprise, some of them stopping outside the compound to admire Naim's handiwork. Early one evening, an entire patrol came inside to look at the work going on in the apartment. "Nice place you have here, Abu Aker," the officer said to Naim. "How much is it costing you?" The officer knew that compounds like the Abu Akers' often represented a family's life savings. Demolishing Palestinian houses had become common practice during the Intifada, not only as another form of collective punishment but also as a literal effort to get to Palestinians where they lived. Even a gesture as benign as inspecting the Abu Akers' rehab work was another form of violating domestic space that had become increasingly fundamental to occupation policy. Soldiers could simply walk right in: *su casa es mi casa*.

It was the same officer who a week earlier had personally announced a curfew on the anniversary of Mohammad's death, a day on which the Abu Akers and their friends had planned a large commemorative feast. The night before, Abu Akram had slaughtered and dressed three sheep. That morning, a group of women were cooking large pots of lamb and rice in the courtyard, and schoolboys were lining up small chairs against the wall just across from the new patio. They had earlier formed a bucket brigade to move a pile of sand from the area designated for Rafat's kitchen to make more room for the guests who would be arriving to pay their respects and join the feasting. Obviously looking for an excuse, the officer had walkie-talkied Bethlehem military headquarters to report the congregating of the young boys. On completing his call, the officer sarcastically reported the decision: "In the name of the Abu Akers and in honor of their son Mohammad, we are clamping a curfew on Deheishe Camp."

When the same officer admired the work being done on the new apartment, Malka pointed out the irony: "A week ago you ruined our feast for Mohammad, and now you want to congratulate us on the work we are doing for our other son. What kind of man are you?"

"I am only doing my job," the officer had said.

Like house demolitions, home invasions served the same policy of getting to the Palestinians where they lived. Soldiers entered houses without search warrants on the pretext of looking for youths on the wanted list. Sometimes the soldiers had been alerted to the presence of "Bingo" youths by collaborators keeping watch on their neighbors' comings and goings; sometimes patrols were doing a sweep of an area following a demonstration or a Molotov cocktail incident; other times, it would seem, a group of bored men needed to find a way of amusing themselves.

During the two years that Mohammad stayed alive after he was shot, I witnessed four out of the dozens of times that soldiers walked right into the Abu Akers' house. I was part of a fifth invasion on my second return visit to Deheishe. That I was on the scene during these invasions no doubt kept to a minimum the kind of destruction I found when I visited a martyr's household in the Christian quarter of Jerusalem's Old City only weeks after I arrived on the West Bank in the summer of 1988. Up to that time, the young martyr, sixteen-year-old Nidal Rabbadi, was one of only two Christians who had been fatally shot during the uprising. The first, Khader Elias Tarazi, had been a teenager in Gaza City; soldiers had displayed his body across their jeep, his arms extended in the manner of crucifixion. I had visited the boy's mother about a year after his death, and she was still heartbroken. Less than a year later, she would die of natural causes, a woman in her early forties.

"He was a very good Christian," Khader's mother kept saying to me as she looked across the room to a framed picture of the Virgin Mary sitting on top of the television set. The fact that he was a believer somehow precluded for her any possibility of his being a stone thrower. Or that soldiers could kill him. She was still having trouble making sense of his death.

As soon as I entered the Rabbadis' Old City apartment, I saw evidence of the army's invasion on the day after the funeral. Books were strewn throughout the hallway, furniture had been overturned, the television was smashed in the salon, and flour and rice were dumped on the kitchen floor. A downstairs relative's apartment was being used to receive mourners, but its occupants were nervous about the soldiers' threatened return.

The first of the invasions I witnessed at the Abu Akers' took place very soon after Mohammad had returned home from his first months of hospitalization. News of a Molotov cocktail incident reached us about ten o'clock that night. The Molotov had exploded down on the main Hebron-Jerusalem Road, and the family immediately prepared for the house-to-house searches they knew would begin within the hour.

Malka and Naim turned out all the lights except for the one in the hallway between the kitchen and bathroom. Hala and her grandmother were already asleep in the back bedroom, and Mohammad had just hooked himself up to his intravenous feeding machine. He was lying awake on his bed, the machine at his side. Nida' stationed herself at a back window facing the road to watch for army patrols. I was motioned silently toward the bedroom I was using, next to Mohammad's, and given one of Malka's long nightdresses to put on over my clothes.

A large group of *shabab* had been at the house earlier in the evening. Those still remaining went into hiding along with Nidal and Rafat. Before he disappeared, Nidal told me that I was what stood between him and prison. At that time, he and another of the youths were on the wanted list. I told him I would do my best but, new to the experience, I had little idea of what to expect.

Within the hour, soldiers pounded on the outside gate. Naim went out to unlock it, and two of the patrol came with him into the house and stood at the doorway to the bedroom section, both hands on their M-16s. As though we had rehearsed it in advance, I appeared in my nightgown just as Malka turned on Mohammad's light so that the soldiers could get a good look at the machine and connecting tube that made graphic Mohammad's inability to throw Molotovs. "My son is very sick," she told the soldiers. "He needs his sleep."

Just as the two soldiers were taking note of Mohammad's medical equipment, I asked, "What's the problem?" English was the only weapon I had, and I would be using that question as an opening shot on many occasions. If I managed to ask the question before the soldiers had had a chance to realize there was an American on the scene, the surprise could be disarming.

We were lucky that first time. The two soldiers were obviously young recruits rather than the seasoned Druze who, we learned the next day, had wreaked their usual havoc in neighboring houses. Instead of throwing their weight around, our soldiers had simply said "shalom" and then left.

The second invasion took place one Sunday afternoon the following July when there was neither time nor places enough to hide for the large group of youths gathered in the Western-style salon. The gate having inadvertently been left unlocked, three soldiers suddenly entered the front door of the house. This time my opening question was lost in the commotion. An officer ordered the youths out on the balcony to stand against the wall of the house, arms held high, while they were being searched.

Another soldier checked their identity cards against a computerized wanted list he carried with him.

Mohammad insisted on going out onto the balcony first. I was motioned outside as well when I stood watching Mohammad from the doorway. I said that I was one of his doctors as he lifted his shirt to expose the multiple surgery scars on his abdomen. After checking my passport, the officer asked what kind of doctor I was. "A doctor of philosophy," I said with a smile.

The officer responded in English, but without humor. "I don't have much time for philosophy these days. Why are you here in the camp?"

"Because Mohammad is a special person," I responded. And when he asked why I thought so, I simply said, "Because he is still alive. He should have died the morning he was shot nearly a year ago."

Another set of exchanges began:

"Do you know why he was shot? Do you know there's another side to this situation?" I took the officer up on neither question. Instead I said, "I love this boy and I don't want anything to happen to him." Imagine having an argument with an army officer during a Sunday-afternoon home invasion, bullet magazine and teargas canister strapped to his waist and automatic rifles held ready by his soldiers!

Soldiers came a third time in early fall. Nine youths were gathered in the Abu Aker living room, but there was time enough for all of them to vanish. Khaled, however, volunteered to stay. Suspicions might be raised in a house entirely empty of youths at the noon hour. While the others knew their names to be on the wanted list, Khaled was not sure and he was willing to take his chances.

Three soldiers entered the house this time. I kept stealing glances at one of them. He was as young and appeared to be as unseasoned as the two who had come the night of the Molotov incident. But the expression on this soldier's face was frozen. His mouth and jaw were set, his eyes squinted, and he stared straight ahead. He seemed an extension of the M-16 he kept at the ready. Behind the rigid expression, I tried somehow to imagine a young man with whom I might be talking philosophy over Arabic coffee under other circumstances. No words passed between us, however, not even my usual question. There seemed no possibility of penetrating his mask of hatred or fear.

When the soldiers left, the rest of the youths reappeared. They hooted and cuffed Khaled with their mock congratulations on his not being "Bingo." Where I come from, bingo is played in church basements. The first one to call out the word picks up a prize. In Deheishe, however, being "Bingo" picks up six months of administrative detention in the Negev Desert, where one freezes in winter and cooks in summer.

I have already described the fourth and fifth invasions. The fourth sent Mohammad back to Makassad Hospital two days after he had been discharged following emergency gall bladder surgery. The fifth home invasion happened on the eve of Id al-Adha while we were out on the roof eating the sautéed liver of the lamb slaughtered for the feast commemorating Abraham's substitute for the sacrifice of Ishmael.

Although it was not a house invasion, an incident on this current visit brought things even closer to home since it had specifically to do with me. During the third curfew that had been imposed in response to stone throwing, I decided to sneak out of the camp to see friends in Jerusalem. I probably could have secured permission to leave, but I did not want to call additional attention to my presence in the camp after I had made my own sarcastic comments about Israel's "preemptive strike policy" to the officer who announced the curfew late on the morning of the anniversary celebration the family and friends had been planning. The officer had announced the curfew shortly after he ordered the young boys out of the road.

"Are you making one of Israel's famous preemptive strikes?" I had asked the officer, making reference to a pattern of past behaviors—like the 1967 and 1982 attacks, respectively, against Syria and Lebanon—justified by Israel as "security" measures. "Do the ten- and twelve-year-old 'terrorists' make you nervous?"

I succeeded in sneaking out of the camp that morning, but I was seen coming back in later in the afternoon by another officer and three of his men who were stationed on a rooftop near the stone factory entrance. The officer signaled for me to stop and then came down with one of the other soldiers who kept his hands on his automatic rifle. He was angry not so much because I had broken the curfew, but because I had not asked his permission to leave.

"After all, I have a mind I can use," he had said angrily. "I am perfectly capable of saying yes to people like you even though I say no to the others." I did not correct his double category mistake, which not only placed me against the "others" but also presumed to align me with himself. I was already nervous enough about the possibility of being barred from reentering the camp.

As a result of my being caught, nine soldiers came looking for me at the Abu Aker house twenty-eight hours later. The same officer pounded on the Abu Akers' gate about eight o'clock that night. "Where is the American woman?" the officer asked Malka when she opened the gate. "Does she stay with you?"

I had told the officer that I was visiting friends in the camp when he asked me why I was trying to get in under the curfew. "I'm staying at the Abu Akers' house," I had said. "You know about their son Mohammad, don't you?" He had quickly replied, "I know about everyone in Deheishe."

I was on the other side of the camp visiting Nasser when the soldiers came that evening. Malka, Nida', and Hala rushed over to tell me about the incident. Hala was wide-eyed, and even Nida' was excited.

"It is normal," Nasser tried to assure me. "The soldiers just want to let you know they can come to see you anytime they want. It happens all the time."

From that night until I left for the States about two weeks later, I was aware of every foot I put in front of the other. Even after I had been assured by an UNRWA refugee affairs officer that I was breaking no law to be staying in the camp unless it were declared a closed military area, I felt the need to be supercautious, ducking my head if I happened to be on the balcony when a patrol passed on the other side of the compound wall and dashing into a neighbor's house if I spotted soldiers ahead of me.

The two-week effort to be careful was exhausting. That Palestinians had had for so long to suppress a level of fear whose duration and depth went so far beyond my own astonished me. I was able for the first time to appreciate at my own gut level the courage they had to muster to keep living their daily lives. Malka's sister-in-law's continuing to cross-stitch during a house invasion, for instance, was an act even more daring than I at first had imagined. To think again about Anwar's risking death for a marble game left me speechless.

The series of curfews, five of them during my third return, was triggered by stone throwing. But this time, stone throwing was a response not only to the Israeli Occupation but also to a new set of Palestinian tactics that had been inspired by Dr. Abdul-Shafi's plenary speech in Madrid. "Today," he had said, "our people under occupation are holding high the olive branch of peace." Shortly after his speech of October 31, 1991, a new kind of demonstration suddenly emerged. Youths in Ramallah began handing out olive branches to Israeli soldiers. Overnight, the new demonstrations spread north and south to Jenin and Jerusalem. On the fifth day of the Madrid Conference, November 4, olive branches began appearing in Deheishe. They were carried by youth groups who supported Arafat's Fatah, the party that led the Palestinian delegation at the Madrid peace talks. The camp's Popular Front supporters, however, had already devised a countertactic to a gesture they regarded to be as empty as the talk about peace.

"Peace is more than good feeling," Nidal had said. "The army being presented with olive branches is the same army that killed two people in Hebron on the second day of the conference. This is no time for olive branches. It is the time to continue our stone throwing."

Popular Front supporters decided to abort any effort at organizing on the part of the olive-branchers. By using stones to trigger a general curfew in the camp, they could keep the Fatah youth, along with the rest of the camp, out of the streets. For the most part, the countertactic was successful except in the case of a small band of little boys who, shouting "Salaam!" at the top of their lungs, carried sad little branches that looked like they came off a Middle East version of Charlie Brown's Christmas tree. Even at that, a patrol was soon hot on their heels.

Despite the transformative activity inside and out, spirits were noticeably lower by the time I returned to Deheishe for the anniversary of Mohammad's death. As a result of losing Palestinian remittances from the Gulf states, the West Bank economy had grown even worse. Israel's farms and businesses and particularly its proliferating settlements offered the only source of work for the Deheishe *shabab* who were eager to marry and otherwise get on with their lives. Since I had last visited, even Nidal had put in several months of work on a settlement near Ramallah.

"My friends and I joke about it," he told me. "We tell one another to build strong houses for the Soviet Jews, since these places will be part of our state one day."

But the prospects for statehood were diminishing by the day as the opening of the Madrid peace conference drew closer. Nidal and his friends were not optimistic about its outcome. "It is an American conference, not an international conference," Nidal said. "The Arabs now have no power to take, and America will not force Israel to give." His worst fears about an imposed Desert Storm settlement seemed to be coming true. More than that, he feared that the Arab governments would use Palestinian participation in the peace talks to rid themselves of the Palestinian problem altogether: "When the Palestinians fail to get self-determination, these governments will say that since we agreed to come to the conference, we must live with the outcome."

Another of the friends, Hussein, offered a further reason for their dejection: "Peace talks will only give more life to a now-sick Israel. Without the conference, Israel will continue to suffer from its own weak economy and internal fighting." Peace talks would serve only to prop things up again. Nasser maintained that the Palestinians had been backed into a corner by U.S. Secretary of State James Baker's repeated admonition that the Madrid talks were their last chance for peace. "The bus is stopping now, but it won't stop again," Baker had been warning. Nasser, however, used his own analogy: "It is easy to enter the door, but not so easy to get out, especially if you find yourself in a room with a lion and a snake." Under arrangements that conceded so much to Israel's demands, peace talks could further isolate the Palestinians by delivering legitimacy to Israel and freezing the status quo. The talks could not be taking place at a worse time. "After the Gulf War," Nasser said, "Palestinians have no room at all and are living in the dark."

Nasser accompanied me on a visit to one of his neighbors, an elderly man then in ill health who was the father of the only Palestinian peace delegate currently living in a refugee camp. His son, Saleh Abu-Laban, had been released in the large Israeli-Palestinian prisoner exchange in 1985 after serving fifteen years of a life sentence for his political activity. When I asked the father, a retired sheikh, how he felt about his son's participation in the peace talks, the old man's answer was circumspect: "I would rather that my son be in Madrid than back in prison."

Even more than they were troubled by the looming peace talks, Nidal and his friends were upset by several collaboration incidents in Deheishe over that summer. Since 1967, when a system of collaboration had become crucial to Israel's control over the territories it had won from Jordan and Egypt, Palestinian collaborators had been responsible for "many of the worst abuses meted out by the [Israeli] military," according to Mouin Rabbani, a doctoral student in Middle East history at the University of Durban. During the first two years of the uprising, collaborators were directly responsible for the killing of at least seven people, including a boy of five, a mother of ten children, and a man in his seventies, according to al-Haq, the West Bank affiliate of the International Commission of Jurists. Stories of betrayal, violence, vandalism, and humiliation at the hands of collaborators abound. Earlier in the summer, the older brother of one of Mohammad's friends had been exposed as a collaborator. Two years earlier, Mohammad's friend, the sixteen-year-old Nasser, had been one of the three martyrs killed on successive days during Ramadan. The martyr's mother, who had responded to the death of her teenage son with the strongest of voices about the injustice of the Palestinian situation, was now near the breaking point as a result of the humiliation caused by her other son's activity. A family that formerly had been elevated to a place of honor in the camp was now a family that had to lower its head.

In addition to this case, there was a second case of alleged collaboration that ended in the death of the accused, a twenty-two-year old Deheishe resident who was suspected of having been recruited by the Mossad while he was studying in Egypt. Around the time the young man's body was found in a mountainous area outside the camp, a close friend of the *shabab* disappeared. A brother-in-law of the suspected collaborator, he had taken it upon himself as a matter of family honor to present the young man for interrogation. Since then he was nowhere to be seen. There was talk about his having had to go far away from the area, leaving behind his wife and newborn son. The *shabab* were upset by the death, the first incident of its kind in Deheishe, and sad that their friend was likely to be gone for a long time. All aspects of the event had badly shaken the people I talked to.

The third of the summer's collaboration cases involved a youth I knew, a close friend of Mohammad's younger brother, Hazem, who had treated the Abu Akers' house as a second home. I had seen him often, a young teenager hanging out like others his age. Although Yasser's infractions were minor relative to the proven activity of the first collaborator and the alleged activity of the second, his case was especially unsettling to the *shabab* because it had come so close to home. There was no specific mention of what Yasser had done except to have kept an eye open and an ear cocked for general information. Like other low-level informants, he had been recruited by a slightly more senior Palestinian collaborator in exchange for money and sex as well as having the way paved for his getting a taxi-driving permit from Bethlehem military government headquarters. Securing the permits that are required by the military government for everything from taking driving lessons to adding a room to one's house and, in Yasser's case, driving a taxi often requires a willingness to inform on one's neighbors.

Yasser's infractions having been minor, the punishment was light. The *shabab* required him only to make a public confession after which he could return to normal life. Yasser's own family, however, imposed a stiffer sentence. They required that he stay inside the house for three months. In virtual solitary confinement, he would be permitted no visitors. I happened to be in the Abu Akers' veranda the first time he went out in the camp. I saw him walking down to the main road accompanied by his mother, an aunt, and one of his brothers. Malka told me he was probably going to military headquarters to renew his identity card.

Until the summer of 1991, Deheishe collaboration had largely been contained or kept at the low level of petty informants outside the party structure by the threat of losing a place within the system of solidarity that had defined the camp's special character for a decade or more. Deheishe solidarity was special not only in the residents' own view but also in the estimation of many other West Bankers who were aware of Deheishe's history of resistance—bus drivers, for example, who often refused payment from those getting on at the camp entrance. To lose one's place was tantamount to losing one's selfhood.

This solidarity was being tested in the extreme over the summer of 1991. As Deheishe residents came more clearly to realize, the real danger of collaboration lay not so much in what it could do for Israeli intelligence or even in the additional physical harm to which collaborators armed by the Shin Bet exposed the Palestinian population. Rather, its gravest danger lay in the wedge it inserted among Palestinians themselves. If suspicion of one another came to rule the day, the struggle would self-destruct. Wedges the Intifada had succeeded in dislodging— wedges that for more than twenty years had successfully been inserted between city and village, refugees and businesspersons, Muslim and Christian, even Muslim and Muslim in Israel's support for the Muslim Brotherhood in the 1960s when that Islamic organization had posed a serious threat to Egypt's President Nasser—were once again being reinserted. This time they were being driven between and even within Palestinian political parties by means of increasing use of collaboration, an instrument of the enemy that, in turning Palestinians against one another could be more destructive than bullets or beatings.

I was visiting Deheishe when Ibrahim, a twenty-four-year-old collaborator, showed up outside the house of the twins Ya'coub and Ishaq. It was about 1:30 in the morning during the second week of my postwar visit in June 1991. Ibrahim was the brother of Abdel Azziz, a young man who was part of our spring promenades. Abdel Azziz and his family had disowned Ibrahim, who was paid and armed by the Shin Bet and had even gone over the Green Line—the boundary between Israel and the West Bank—to live in an area protected by the Israeli security service.

Ibrahim had had his gun on him when he shouted that early morning for Ishaq, a small and exceptionally quiet young man who had been able to elude camp patrols for nearly four years. Knowing all the escape routes, Ishaq had taken refuge in other homes, and, before the army began carrying photographs of all the wanted youths, had successfully used false identity cards. Ishaq was carrying a false card when he was finally arrested by the Shin Bet in August 1991 at Hamdi Faraj's Bethlehem Press Office.

Ibrahim shouted that he had money for Ishaq and then climbed a wall to break into the house. Ya'coub came outside in his sleeping shorts and told Ibrahim to leave. Instead, the collaborator climbed down and, in a parodic inversion of the biblical story of Jacob and the angel, he began wrestling with Ya'coub. Before Ibrahim had a chance to use his gun, Ya'coub was arrested by an army patrol waiting just around the corner.

Like so many male collaborators in the region, Ibrahim was recruited as a boy while he was at al-Fara'a prison, where thirteen- and fourteen-year-old youths were detained and then interrogated after regular round-ups. Twenty kilometers northeast of the West Bank town of Nablus, al-Fara'a was built by the British as an army camp during Palestine's Mandate period and continued to serve that purpose under the Jordanians. Its buildings were not used by Israel from 1967 until the spring of 1982, when it became a prison known as Fara'a Correction Center.

Since January 1984, it had operated as an interrogation center used mainly to impose a form of intimidation and humiliation that, like other methods of collective punishment such as curfews, house demolitions, school closings, and the withdrawal of basic services from entire villages or camps, was intended to control the West Bank population, particularly males between the ages of sixteen and thirty-five. Called *tirtur* in Hebrew, the al-Fara'a treatment of detainees included hooding, beating, detention in toilet areas and cells flooded with water, sleep and food deprivation, forced braying and barking, and, in the case of young detainees, being ordered to masturbate in front of interrogators. The following affidavit was given by a fifteen-year-old Deheishe resident whose interrogation ended after he finally confessed to throwing stones at an Israeli car:

At exactly 1:30 on the night of January 22nd, 1984 four border guard patrol vehicles and a car from the intelligence forces came to the house [in Deheishe Camp]. They banged threateningly on the door and when it was opened they proceeded to search the room I was living in. They found nothing, but informed me of an order for my arrest. I was taken to the main street and from there to the Bassa center [military headquarters] in Bethlehem. I was there for half an hour, and during this time the soldiers there beat me without any justification. Then I was moved to al-Fara'a prison with three other youths from Deheishe Camp.

When I got to al-Fara'a, my personal possessions were taken and I went to the doctor's room for a check—I didn't have any illness—and was taken from there to the Stable [where the British once housed their horses]. There, I was handcuffed with one hand over my shoulder and the other behind my back, and they put a sack over my head. Then they took me into the toilets where they forced me to sit down in the water. I stayed there for two days. During this time I was subjected to ugly methods of interrogation; they beat me with electricity cables and ordered me to turn round and round for a long time so that I got giddy and nauseous. They made me stand cross-like [arms outstretched] in the middle of the interrogation room for an hour and a half, after which I simply wasn't aware of what was happening to me, as I was in a heavy faint due to the interrogation.

When I came to, I found a nurse beside me calling me by name. He gave me some tablets. Half an hour later I was taken back to interrogation. They used extremely unpleasant techniques of interrogation; they kicked me with their army boots on my shins, and used insults and bad language, saying for instance that they were going to bring my sister and do what they liked with her. This went on for a long time. I told them I was innocent, but they didn't believe me and kept on torturing me for twelve days. During this period, many charges were made against me, but I only confessed to one, which was throwing stones at a car with Israeli number plates.

After twelve days they put me in the rooms [nine rooms located in the main buildings of the prison; each one is twenty meters square, holds up to thirty persons, and contains no toilets]. I stayed there for two months. During these two months, I was taken to court four times, and on my fifth appearance was sentenced. The judge was satisfied with my term of detention (two months) and sentenced me to two months suspended for three years. I was released at 7:30 in the evening on March 22nd, 1984.[1]

The al-Fara'a form of *tirtur* represents what the report from which this excerpt was taken goes on to suggest is "a system designed to break the spirit of any detainee . . . regardless of whether or not he committed any act against the occupation."[2] The report does not go on to say what is also well known—that the treatment is designed to pressure younger boys into collaboration.

Two years after the fifteen-year-old's affidavit, Mohammad Abu Aker had been interrogated at al-Fara'a on his first detention. He also was fifteen. Nidal was fourteen when he was first taken to the interrogation center. He told me he spent most of his eighteen days, the usual period of interrogation without charges, with a cloth sack over his head. Water would be poured on the sack, and, handcuffed to an overhead pipe in near-freezing January temperatures, he would have to stand in front of fans the whole night, sometimes in the nude. Recordings of screams would periodically be played over a loudspeaker.

Young Deheishe boys like him would be questioned not so much for information as to push them into usually minor confessions that could then be used to blackmail them into the first stage of collaborating. Those who broke under interrogation feared most of all the loss of standing with their camp comrades, a fear that the Shin Bet could use to its own advantage. In exchange for a promise of secrecy about their initial confession, boys like the young Ibrahim would be recruited for continuing collaboration work and be hailed as heroes—for remaining "strong" under harsh interrogation—when they returned to the camp.

Preparing boys for interrogation as soon as they entered their teens had long been a Deheishe rite of passage. These boys were provided detailed descriptions of the torture they could expect at centers like al-Fara'a along with repeated admonitions about the importance of maintaining a code of silence. Some of the *shabab* more recently admitted that preparation had been weak at the emotional level. To the instructions given beforehand, there should have been added a debriefing session after a boy was released. "He should be encouraged to admit in confidence any mistakes he has made," one of Nidal's friends, a young man who wanted to continue graduate work in special education when and if he could find the money, told me. "After all," Burhan said, "they are still children, even though we expect them to be strugglers."

My instruction about the ins and outs of collaboration went even further during this anniversary visit. I learned about the various levels of punishment meted out to Deheishe collaborators under a system of strict rules. The collaborators who are well known to everyone—who are "burned," in British cold war intelligence parlance for "identified"—are usually ignored. Often they are old and live otherwise normal lives within the community like the father of Nazzem, who ran a soft drink supply business out of his garage in the camp. Nazzem was the youth who had been dying from a plastic bullet in his brain when Mohammad left for Boston the first time. His was one of the three martyrs' families we visited the day after Mohammad returned home from his months of hospitalization.

Other collaborators, like a woman who lived across the street from the Abu Akers, represented another level of danger to the camp. She was known to sleep around, and the marginality of her life made her especially vulnerable to pressures that could easily step up her collaborative activity. Her threat to the community's security having somehow to be contained, a "strike force," a group assigned by their particular political party, was called on to set limits on the woman's behavior—first through a series of warnings and then, when the warnings were ineffective, through beating. In camp vernacular, these masked youths were known collectively as Abu Kees or, ironically, "father of the sack," the sack that was placed over detainees' heads during Shin Bet interrogation.

Harsh treatment of "line-crossing" women has a long history in the Middle East, where patriarchal traditions have placed upon women the burden of family honor. As Moroccan sociologist Fatima Mernissi has demonstrated, uncontained female sexuality represents a potentially destabilizing social force (*fitna*) in response to which Islamic family law was established not so much to contain the unmarried pubescent female as to shield society from a power of otherness that might run amok. The veil is meant to protect what is beyond it, Mernissi argues, not what is behind it.[3]

The harsh treatment of the neighbor woman, obviously open to charges of sexism and misogyny, can be understood at the same time as action necessary to counter and contain the fallout of *political fitna* so ready to be unleashed by the pervasively destabilizing effects of the collaboration system. Maintaining boundaries—or at least withstanding their constant violation—has been of paramount importance to the people of Deheishe in continuing to live under conditions in which solidarity is a matter of survival.

While women have been the overseers and primary maintainers of the dailiness that has been at the heart of Deheishe's struggle, they continue to be vulnerable, even in a secular, non-Islamic setting, to being co-opted into collaboration by an Occupation policy that, by manipulating a traditional code of honor, turns women, especially single and uneducated women, into perpetrators as well as victims of violation. Instances of moral entrapment, known as *isqat*, include the secret photographing of young women in various states of undress while they are trying on clothes in dress shops. That these photos (with the threat of showing them around) can be used to blackmail them into collaboration, often in the form of prostitution, demonstrates the extent to which civil society continues to be shaped by the *doxa* of honor, a fact not lost on Israel's collaborator recruitment tactics carried out in al-Fara'a as well as in the shops of Nablus, East Jerusalem, and Bethlehem.

The worst form of punishment until now, a form of shunning, is reserved for those who are discovered infiltrating the party structure. In extreme cases, this punishment involves expulsion from the West Bank altogether. Always it includes being disowned by the family. Even though the collaborator might remain in the home, he or she is restricted to a single room, forbidden even to look out the window. In essence, such a collaborator is sentenced to solitary confinement and deprived of Deheishe solidarity.

To kill collaborators, as might have happened to the young man who died under interrogation, would represent a big change in Deheishe. As demonstrated by the fate of Jewish collaborators in World War II and black collaborators in the townships of apartheid South Africa, this more extreme form of punishment in situations demanding solidarity for survival (and where the official court system offers no possibility of redress) would not be unprecedented.

Having come so close to home, collaboration that summer had put everyone on the alert. No one was any longer above suspicion, even activist families like the Abu Akers. This bleak situation was made even worse by an economy that forced another kind of collaboration with the enemy: helping to build Jewish settlements on or near land that had once belonged to Deheishe family members who had fled in 1948 and 1967. In addition to the upcoming peace talks, which most Deheishe residents opposed, their own collaborative activity threatened to sabotage any dream of statehood. Demoralization finally seemed to be getting a grip on the camp.

Nidal and his friends knew very well that giving in to demoralization would mark the ultimate success of Occupation policy. That fact explains why it had been so important for them to plan special events to commemorate the anniversary of Mohammad's death, a martyrdom that even before Mohammad actually died—his "living martyrdom"—had strengthened Deheishe's resolve to carry on its decades-old resistance activity. That Mohammad had become a revolutionary icon for his people also explained why it was just as important to the Israeli military that a curfew be clamped on the camp that day.

In addition to collaboration, the summer's united leadership decisions within the Intifada itself were creating problems for Deheishe *shabab*. An Intifada leaflet that April gave such latitude to Palestinian businesses that occupation seemed once again to be approaching a normal way of life: shops could stay open until three o'clock instead of closing at one. On mourning days they could stay open between eight and eleven o'clock in the morning instead of closing for three days straight. Shops inside Jerusalem's Old City were given even more business hours: they could stay open daily until five o'clock and, beginning April 23, they could keep evening hours every Thursday. With business-as-almost-usual returning to the West Bank, Nidal and his friends thought the Intifada was in danger of betraying itself.

Such betrayal was beyond the imagination of someone as single-minded as the Abu Akers' young neighbor, Joffer. He might have been one of the children David Grossman had written about after visiting a Deheishe kindergarten one day in 1986, when Joffer would have been five. Already Grossman could foresee their growing up to be fighters. I met Joffer two years later, when he was seven. I asked him then what he wanted to be when he grew up. He immediately laid three fingers on his left shoulder to indicate that he wanted to be a Palestinian army officer.

"But what if there is peace?" I put to him. He just grinned and shrugged his shoulders.

Joffer had turned ten when I saw him on my third visit to the camp. Over the three years I knew him, Joffer spent as much time at the Abu Akers' as he did in his own house just across the road. I had come to nickname him Hiss-hiss, the name that Deheishe residents give to the ever-present mosquitos whose bites leave a sharp burning sensation. Like them, Joffer made his presence all too known. There were times I locked myself in my bedroom to escape his practical jokes—trying to grab the live electrical wire next to the veranda window, for example—and exasperating behavior such as his frantic search through my suitcase for a T-shirt commemorating my hometown centennial like the one I brought for Hala. His irritating "How are you?" at every turn (he was endlessly practicing his few words of English) drove me up more than one wall over those years.

The fact that Joffer was always underfoot meant that the Abu Akers sent him on errands when Hala was sulking or just not around. Joffer was always willing to get a pack of Imperial cigarettes for Nidal, a sack of potatoes for Malka, or shampoo for Nida'. Ordering fresh chickens, buying a ten-roll package of toilet paper, being a forward scout for *shabab* who wanted to avoid army patrols—Joffer was on call for any and all of it. David Grossman was correct in seeing runny-nosed children like him as future Molotov cocktail throwers.

Mohammad must have been seeing the same thing when one of the two names he gave his dropper machine was Joffer. In addition to being committed to the struggle, Joffer was, like the machine, impossible to get rid of. At the same time, however, Mohammad had to acknowledge the fact that the dropper machine that made possible his nightly infusions of liquid nutrition was his life source. Without it, he would die. Without the upcoming generation of Joffers, so Mohammad must have believed, Palestinians' hope for their future could not survive. In fact, the other name Mohammad gave to his machine was Amal, the Arabic word for hope. Between the two of them, Joffer and Amal, Mohammad was able to put up with the otherwise depressing fact of the cold technology on which his second life depended. Like Joffer, the machine was a pest; but also like the young struggler, it was indispensable.

The blood of martyrdom has carried enormous weight for both Christians and Muslims since the deaths of Jesus and the Prophet Mohammad's grandson Hussein, who was killed in battle in the year 680. While Christians remember Jesus' death by the drinking of his blood, the dramatic reenactment of Hussein's martyrdom has served as the yearly "passion play" for Shia Muslims.

For the predominantly Sunni Muslim population on the West Bank, martyrdom is linked to the land, as suggested by the roots in the heroic drawing of Mohammad. At the same time religious and political, individual and communal, historical and eschatological, the meaning of Palestinian martyrdom lies between loss and recovery. The blood of martyrdom promises to restore continuity—all but obliterated in the catastrophic events of 1948 and 1967—between past and future.

Ironically, martyrdom goes hand in hand with insisting on living a fully human life. "We must live our life" finally means inhabiting a "homeland" where, enriched by martyrs' blood, the objects of memory can combine with the objects of desire. More than a piece of geography, the homeland is a construct of the collective political-poetic imagination. Far from being an abstraction, the homeland is of "one flesh and bone" with the Palestinians, as Mahmoud Darwish insists in his poem "Diary of a Palestinian Wound": "Mount Carmel is in us," he writes, and "on our eyelashes" is the "grass of Galilee." Such embodiment of the homeland would make redundant a literal Palestinian return to the mountain above Haifa and the "grass of Galilee." In their imagination, the Palestinians are already there. Martyrdom has been their symbolic passport.

Darwish, the composer of the 1988 Palestinian Declaration of Independence, resigned from the PLO executive committee in opposition to the Gaza-Jericho agreement, which he, like many Deheishe residents, sees as a betrayal of the martyrs' blood. "I see multitudes of families waiting on the shore," Darwish wrote in response to the agreement. "They are the two generations of martyrs. We walked them to their deaths in the struggle for Palestine. They stand there waiting for the ship of the PLO, but the ship has disappeared."[4]

Deheishe residents have reduced the agreement to *fil-fil* and *moz*, the red pepper and banana for which Gaza and Jericho have become famous. Whether Mohammad Abu Aker's life, along with the lives of the other Deheishe martyrs, will be too high a price for the "Gaza and Jericho First" agreement is a question that Joffer and the children of the stones will not be asking. For them, it is only a question of what form their own generation of struggle will take.

Epilogue

Crossing Borders

Differences do not only exist between outsider and insider—two entities. They are also at work within the outsider herself, or the insider herself—a single entity. She who knows she cannot speak of them without involving her story, also knows that she cannot make a gesture without activating the to and fro movement of life.
—Trinh T. Minh-ha

I envy Jean Genet's autobiographical confidence in *Prisoner of Love*. In telling his story about the two years he spent with a group of Palestinian fighters in Jordan, Genet seemed to know exactly what to show of his own profile and what to keep in the shadows: "Never from the front," he writes, "with my age and stature apparent." Instead Genet appears "either in three-quarter or half-profile or from the back." He was able to "reconstruct [his] size and position in the group," he says, only "from the pattern of a cigarette moved downwards, a lighter upward."[1]

How much of myself I needed, dared, and presumed to show (and from what angles) was for me an ongoing and often unsettling question in the writing of this book. About what might be called the problematic of positionality, Pierre Bourdieu writes:

One's relationship to the social world and to one's proper place in it is never more clearly expressed than in the space and time one feels entitled to take from others: more precisely, in the space one claims with one's body in physical space, through a bearing and gestures that are self-assured or reserved, expansive or constricted . . . and with one's speech in time, through the interaction time one appropriates and the self-assured or aggressive, careless or unconscious way one appropriates it.[2]

To insert the question-in-English ("What's the problem?") I asked during home invasions was one thing; to encroach on the space and time belonging to others' stories was something else.

For Trinh T. Minh-ha, professor of women's studies at Berkeley, the problem of othering begins "at home": to make the gesture of speaking about the other, she suggests, is to activate one's own story in the "to and fro movement of life." "Differences do not only exist between outsider and insider—two entities," she writes; these differences "are also at work within the outsider herself, or the insider herself—a single entity."[3] To tell the story (or, as for Genet, *a* story) of the Palestinians has been to cross borders *within* myself as well as *between* myself and them; to tell *their* story has both engaged and enabled the recollecting, reconnecting, and narrativizing of my *own*.

Returning once again to the "to and fro movement" of Genet's autobiographical narrative: that the Palestinians Genet writes about had their actual existence in the real world he had no doubt. But it was in the "somewhere else," he said, that he found the Palestinian mother and son who became for him the "emblem of the Palestinian Revolution." The one night he spent in their house in 1970 became the heart of the book that Genet began to write fourteen years later. Assigned to Hamza's room, Genet was wordlessly served the small cup of Arabic coffee and accompanying glass of water that Hamza's mother customarily brought in to her son at night; when the cup and glass were empty, they were just as silently removed from the darkened room where her son slept when he was at home. Genet writes:

> Because he was fighting that night, I'd taken the son's place and perhaps played his part in his room and his bed. For one night and for the duration of one simple but oft-repeated act, a man older than she was herself became the mother's son. . . . Though younger than I, during that familiar act she was my mother as well as Hamza's. (375)

The lines with which Genet ends his account of that night make clear a lifetime of waiting for a maternal and even sacramental gesture that could offset his experience of childhood abandonment by his own mother, a Parisian prostitute: "It was in my own personal and portable darkness that the door of my room opened and closed. I fell asleep."

At the very end of *Prisoner of Love*, a title that ironically suggests release from lovelessness, Genet, by that point in his life an aficionado of revolutions, writes:

I did the best I could to understand how different this revolution was from others, and in a way I did understand it. But what will remain with me is the night in Irbid where I slept for one night, and fourteen years during which I tried to find out if that night ever happened. (375)

In portraying Hamza and his mother as a kind of Palestinian pietà, Genet momentarily rescues himself from a lifetime of solitary confinement. The healing epiphany of mother and son is testimony to the autobiographical achievement of *Prisoner of Love* as well as to the power of what Genet describes as "the story, a story, of the Palestinians."

That I, too, found healing among the Palestinians, by this point goes without saying. But let me pick up again the story of the little girl who ran to her grandmother's house when the kitchen spoon dropped into emptiness, the second part of the early-memory assignment I had hoped to use in the field-workers' autobiography workshop that never got off the ground:

> From the side yard where I am digging a hole, my memory moves inside my own house on Jefferson Avenue. Downstairs, people have come to view my father's body, laid out along the living room wall closest to the Bozichs'. A little girl is pushing against tall legs to get closer to the casket.
>
> The next thing I know, we—the little girl and I—are both upstairs, memory giving way to a dreamlike scene in which I, now a grown-up, am watching the little girl, who is sitting in the corner of a room bare of furniture and color. One of her arms is hugging her waist, the other arm is over the top of her head. Her legs are folded under her. Two walls intersect behind her, but, holding as still as she can, she leans against neither. Empty space extends in front of her.
>
> I am standing at the edge of that space. She is unaware of my presence and thinks that no one in the world knows where she is. I don't know if she is hiding or waiting to be found. I don't know if the arm that curves over her head is shielding or cradling. I don't know if she is sad, angry, or afraid. She cannot or will not speak. I, too, remain silent.

Forty-five years after my father died, I, by then a tenured university professor, walked down David Street inside the walls of Jerusalem's Old City. It was the fall of 1986, and I had checked into a hospice just inside Jaffa Gate where I planned to stay while finding an apartment for my year of research on Holocaust autobiography. Nothing in those intervening years had prepared me for the sounds, colors, smells, and commotion that suddenly greeted me when I made a turn down stone-paved steps that descended into the Old City's market. As far down as I could see, the narrow street was lined on both sides with open stalls of fresh fruit, silver jewelry, and embroidered robes hanging from shop lintels. No space was empty; no surface was undecorated; nothing was still.

The little girl's excitement momentarily overtook both of us. David Street seemed, at first, to be the world toward which she had dug in her side yard, trusting as children trust that it had to be somewhere. It seemed to be a place where things were enough, where surfaces covered still more surfaces, not empty space. Life was on display for both of us, the professor about to turn fifty and the child she had brought with her to the other side of the world.

By the end of my research year, I knew that Jaffa Gate opened on a scene conforming in myriad ways to the Orientalist expectations, shaped by travel brochures and childhood images of Aladdin and his magic lamp, that Westerners bring with them to the Middle East. I came to realize that the chorus of welcomes from the darkly handsome tradesmen along David Street were meant to tease out dollars. The balding owners, sitting deeper inside their shops, would start off announcing high figures for their unpriced goods; the younger men would then reduce the figure in playful repartee with their mark: "For you, I make a special price," they would say.

Let it be said: David Street business, with few exceptions, was pitched to the middle-aged Western woman. Indeed, David Street was a stage set, designed to the last detail for Orientalist effect. A shrewd way of doing business, I came to appreciate, but no more seductive than Rodeo Drive or Upper Michigan Avenue, where the shop windows of intimate boutiques promise corporate success or eternal sex appeal to young American secretaries and society matrons.

Deheishe Camp was only a half-hour down the road from David Street, but a world of cultural and political difference stood between them. It would take another year for me to learn, for instance, about the collaboration rampant in border areas like Jaffa Gate, the preferred tourist entrance, which intersected the Jewish, Christian, and Muslim quarters of the Old City. And it would take another while for the little girl to reach the true destination she was digging toward from her side yard on Jefferson Avenue.

It was not the exotic that I was in search of all those years. What was lost down the hole was the ordinariness of life, the what-could-go-with-out-saying. I recovered that kitchen spoon in the Palestinian struggle to reconnect their past and future by insisting on maintaining, as the "very content" of their struggle, the realm of domestic dailiness.[4] The combined events of 1948 and 1967, having collectively disconnected an entire people from the daily and the domestic, threatened to sever permanently all connection between past and future in the Palestinian psyche. In December 1987, Palestinians took up stones against a twenty-year occupation that threatened to normalize that set of disconnections.

In joining the company that mourned the death of Mohammad Abu Aker, in commemorating the anniversary of that death as peace talks began in Madrid, and in seeing the martyr's poster held high by Joffer in Rafat's wedding parade and then by Nidal in his wedding a year later, the little girl and I began moving out of the corner. Among a group of exiles who struggled to maintain the ordinariness of their lives, she and I found a world of true plenty. David Street, for all its initial magic, was only a stepping-stone. But it, too, was part of the journey from a mining town in Western Pennsylvania to the West Bank refugee camp where, as Mohammad's mother told me that night on the veranda, I could stop running.

Since 1967, Palestinian domestic space has been violated by land confiscations, house demolitions, and routine home invasions, disruptions, and trashings. Even more invasive and undermining of Palestinian domestic and familial arrangements has been the network of collaborators recruited, protected, and often armed by Israel's security apparatus. More than any other instrument of the Occupation, this collaboration network extended the terrain of state power into the day-by-day "economy of affection," the intricate web of obligation and trust that kept Deheishe residents from falling off the edge of their collective lives.

I was a distraught witness to the profoundly destabilizing effects of another case of suspected collaboration on a fourth return to Deheishe, this one for Rafat's wedding in the early fall of 1992—a two-day ceremony that was the first, apart from Nasser's smaller-scale wedding, to break out of Intifada-imposed restrictions. The otherwise exuberant event was marred not only by the case itself but also by intrafactional disagreement over how to handle it and by the fact that Rafat and Nidal stood on opposite sides of the issue. As a result of tactical disagreements, the Popular Front was facing the possibility of an unprecedented split at both the local and regional levels. That the alleged collaborator was himself an active and trusted Popular Front supporter was bad enough. That he was one of the *shabab* who had lined the back rows of the English, history, and Arabic classes I had visited and, in fact, was one of Nidal's closest friends was profoundly unsettling. Having come to know the young man in the course of veranda gabfests and evening promenades through the camp, I, too, felt shock, pain, and even a sense of betrayal when the name of Mohammad Abu Aker was held up by both sides to legitimize their respective stands on the case.

There seemed no escape from the feuding around me: the reports of fighting between factional groups, the news of old interfamily quarrels being played out in the streets, and, worst of all, the fact of Rafat and Nidal being at one another's throats. I began counting the days until I could fly away. The relentlessly eroding situation both inside and outside the Abu Aker house could not have better served Occupation policy had it been planned. Indeed, Nidal was convinced that it had been: "The Occupation knows our psychology very well," Nidal insisted. "They know that even the slightest rumors about possible collaboration activity can greatly affect our people."[5] Only in planning for the second anniversary commemoration of Mohammad's death several weeks after my departure did the camp begin to bring itself back together again.

Since then, Rafat and his wife have become parents of a second Mohammad Abu Aker, and Nidal the father of a third: Mohammad Rafat and his cousin Mohammad Nidal are living memorials to their martyred uncle. At the time I was finishing this memoir, negotiations under the Oslo Accords ("Gaza-Jericho First") were stalled by the massacre of thirty Palestinians by an American-Jewish zealot during Ramadan prayers in Hebron. In response to international pressure for the protection of Palestinian lives from Hebron's settler population, Israeli negotiators are currently proposing the reinstatement of the Palestinian police force that was forced to resign under charges of collaboration by the Intifada leadership in the early months of the uprising. Deheishe residents continue to oppose a "peace" framework that seems to ensure even more disconnection in what some call the "South Africanization of Palestine" with the dividing of the Occupied Territories into five "Arabstans": the Gaza Strip, the southern West Bank, Jericho, the northern West Bank, and Jerusalem.

In Deheishe's counterstrategy against the old colonial formula of divide and rule, its residents are organizing an election for an interfactional committee to oversee the establishment of a memorial to all the camp's martyrs on land provided by the United Nations. Nidal tells me that the memorial will take the form of a building that will house the plaques, videos, photographs, newspaper articles, banners, and other materials that each martyr's family has been collecting and, until recently, carefully hiding. The building will also be the site of future commemorations, perhaps completed in time for the fourth anniversary of Mohammad Abu Aker's death. Up to now, memorials have usually amounted to little more than a pile of stones at a road side or a grave site, its palm branches drying, its posters tearing or being blown away, its flags being confiscated by soldiers. Deheishe's memories and memorabilia will soon be domiciled in a space of their own, yet another transformation of space—like the spring promenades, the building of the patio, and, I hope, the writing of this memoir—in the service of an emancipatory political domestic.

It is with a final memory of Mohammad and his mother that I end both of my stories, mine and theirs. The memory begins on the morning of a general strike day on March 26, 1989, that protested the signing of the Camp David Accords ten years earlier.[6] The morning afforded me yet another look at the relationship that Mohammad had cultivated with his dropper machine. I had stayed overnight in the camp and woke up to the first round of morning tea. Hala was already in my room combing the blond hair of her doll and dressing it in its wedding outfit. Other rituals followed on course: Nida' helped her grandmother, the *hajeh*, to sit up for her glass of wake-up tea; Naim went off to the gas station, where he would be part of the strike-day skeleton crew; Hazem came in for breakfast from the mountain where he regularly slept to avoid army patrols; Malka momentarily took up her lookout post in the veranda, having already received word of stone throwing from Joffer.

Nidal remained asleep on a mat in the salon during all the commotion. Unsure of whether or not he was "Bingo," he was keeping a low profile those days. For a period of time earlier in the winter, he had slept in a secret unheated burrow, bundled in one of the sleeping bags I bought for him and his friends from an army surplus store in West Jerusalem's Ben Yehuda Mall.

After another round of tea, Malka came back into the salon to plug in the electric baker for the spinach-stuffed triangles she was making for the midafternoon meal. She had already cut up and squeezed the spinach with lemon the night before, so it remained only to make the pastry that morning. She arranged the bowls of flour and water and the cup of oil on the floor between the sleeping Nidal on the far side of the room and the *hajeh* now ensconced in her usual corner chair near the bathroom, a striped blue blanket around her shoulders and her white head covering already sliding to the side. She, Malka, and I would be straightening it for the rest of the day. I sat next to the *hajeh*.

The next family member to join us was Mohammad, who wheeled in his dropper machine from his room down the hallway. He was still attached to the tube that was delivering the last portion of his overnight infusion of protein, acids, minerals, vitamins, and whatever else he needed to stay alive. As his mother was kneading the bread dough, Mohammad stood above her and began to belt out a national song into the dropper machine as though it were the sound system in a recording studio. On finishing the song, he launched into an impassioned speech, scowling and chopping the air like a Japanese Kabuki player.

By the time he finished his lively act, the nutrition bag was empty. He detached the tube from his permanent chest catheter and suddenly dropped onto his mother, unbalancing her and covering her face with kisses. She nearly fell into the large pastry bowl as she beamed the purest pleasure I have ever witnessed. That Palestinian image of mother and son will be the last to fade from my memories of Deheishe, creating ex nihilo a space inaccessible to any oppressor, a space of survival and hope.

Appendix

Excerpted from "The Uprising and the Making of a Hero," Ori Nir, *Ha'aretz*, October 7, 1988. Translated into English for "Selections from the Hebrew Press," Government Press Office Publication, Jerusalem, October 25, 1988.

On Tuesday, October 4, KLM flight 526 en route from Tel Aviv to New York via Amsterdam carried the most admired figure in Deheishe Refugee Camp, located near Bethlehem, on his way to New England Deaconess Hospital in Boston for an intestinal transplant, the success of which is doubtful. Local hero Mohammad Abu Aker, 17, is the most recent link in the chain of myths nurtured by Palestinians in the territories during the uprising. . . .

Abu Aker's friends from Deheishe credit themselves with a considerable portion of his success in the struggle to live. "The guys from the camp bound him to the revolution with an infusion tube," one of them told this reporter. In order to understand the meaning of these comments, one had to see Abu Aker's room: Private, slightly isolated, and located at the end of the hospital's first floor, the room became a sort of Palestinian national shrine. At times it resembled a Marxist-Palestinian propaganda exhibition, and occasionally the Intifada war room. On the wall directly behind the injured youth were hung Palestinian posters dominated by

145

red, black, white and green, colorful miniature Palestinian flags, wood-cuts depicting a map stretching from the Mediterranean sea to the Jordan River, photographs and Palestinian nationalist postcards, and so on. All of this poked out from behind a thicket of tubes and medical instruments, a striking illustration of the process in which Abu Aker has been consolidated into a symbol.

Against this decor lay Abu Aker, usually under the influence of tranquilizers, dazed and thin as a rail, a kind of Palestinian revolutionary icon. Soon the melancholy little room became a site for pilgrimages by camp youth. His close friends, most of whom were well-known to the security services and investigators from the area's detention facilities, took turns sitting at his bedside.

Others, a bit younger, came to the hospital as part of delegations to evince solidarity and provide encouragement. After a few days they began to record Abu Aker, to serve as a posthumous memento. They sought his advice on how to confront soldiers and how to fight, as if they were seeking the advice of an oracle. . . .

The myth has taken hold in this sort of environment. On Monday evening all of Abu Aker's friends came to visit, while a small suitcase containing his and his father Naim's belongings stood in the hospital room, ready for the trip to the U.S. "Most of us appear on the Shin Bet's wanted list," one of them told this reporter, as if in secret. They related deeds spun about him as if they had done so countless times. They said, for example, that Abu Aker always stuck his slingshot in the belt of his trousers; when he was injured on August 6 and fell bleeding, his slingshot slipped to the ground. One of his friends told us that "when they took him to the hospital, he asked us to keep his slingshot for him. After the operation, when he was still groggy from the anesthesia, he repeatedly asked where his slingshot was. We had to bring it to him and place it next to his bed." . . . They also told how Abu Aker withstood torture in a detention facility, how he refused to talk under interrogation, how he became famous even among Shin Bet interrogators, and how he always led every demonstration. "He was admired as a highly skilled fighter even before he was injured," his friend said enthusiastically. "From his hospital bed he taught us how to follow an army patrol and harass it until we succeed in expelling it from the camp."

Excerpted from "Wounded Palestinian Youth in Boston for Hospital Stay," Mary Curtius, *Boston Globe*, October 5, 1988, 3.

Mohammed [*sic*] Abu Aker, a 17-year-old who hopes to undergo a rare intestinal transplant while in Boston, is called a living martyr by many Palestinians.

For almost two months, Abu Aker has been growing weaker after being shot August 6 by an Israeli soldier in Dehaishe [*sic*], a West Bank refugee camp.

As he continued to survive against medical odds, Abu Aker became a human icon for the young men from Dehaishe who counted him as a leader in their war of stones against the Israelis.

Abu Aker, accompanied by his father, arrived at Logan International Airport last night and was taken to New England Deaconess Hospital.

The teen-ager was greeted at Logan by about 30 members of Boston's Arab community, representing most groups. Mostly Palestinians, the well-wishers said they came to show their support for Abu Aker and the Palestinian uprising.

"We are here because we feel a certain amount of pride and commitment to this boy," said Manal Abdulrahman, a spokeswoman for the Association of Arab-American University Graduates, which publishes material supporting Palestinian causes.

Before Abu Aker left for Boston, his room at Jerusalem's Mokassed [*sic*] Hospital had become a shrine. Visitors covered the wall behind his bed with nationalist Palestinian posters and crowded every countertop with floral arrangements.

Daily, dozens and sometimes hundreds of people streamed in to touch him, to hear him speak of his hatred for Israeli control and his devotion to the Palestinian cause. His words were recorded on cassettes, and posters of him were readied in preparation for declaring him a martyr upon his death. The shabab, the militant youths who organize anti-Israeli demonstrations in Dehaishe, traded stories about his bravery and his will to live.

His survival confounded doctors at Mokassad. Struck in the abdomen by what his doctor said was a high-velocity bullet fired at close range, he suffered severe damage to his intestines. He eventually lost all of his small intestine and two-thirds of his large intestine to gangrene, said his doctor, Khaled Qurie.

Since August 29, Abu Aker has survived on hyperalimentation—a treatment that feeds vital nutrients directly into the lower stomach, Qurie said. He grew thinner but remained alert.

"I am very happy to have him still with us," Qurie said, "but I am surprised. He is stable, his vital signs are all right, and his general condition is all right. But he has no small intestine. This is a very unusual case." . . .

The Palestine Human Rights Campaign, an organization based in Chicago, . . . began to coordinate with the Arab-American community in Boston to raise funds and find help for Mohammed, a spokesman for the campaign said during a telephone interview.

"If he had remained in Jerusalem, the alternative was either to let this boy die on his own or to shoot him," said Dr. Anthony Sahyoun, a surgeon at Boston's New England Deaconess. Sahyoun, a Palestinian-American born in Haifa, said he was told of the case by Mokassad doctors who have consulted with him in the past.

"They have no facilities there for this sort of thing," Sahyoun said. He has told fund raisers for Abu Aker that they should try to raise $100,000 for the boy's medical costs.

Sahyoun, interviewed by telephone, said he will have to see the patient before deciding whether an intestinal transplant is feasible. Such a transplant, Sahyoun said, is "still in the experimental stages."

During their 10-month revolt against Israel's military rule in the territories, the Palestinians have elevated many of those killed or imprisoned to the status they call martyrs. Martyrdom feeds a sense among militants in the refugee camps, villages and towns of the territories that their cause is worthy of the ultimate sacrifice.

Notes

Foreword: "Our Blood Will Plant Its Olive Tree"

1. Lila Abu-Lughod, *Writing Women's Worlds: Bedouin Stories* (Berkeley: University of California Press, 1993).
2. Mahmoud Darwish, "The Earth Is Closing in around Us," in *Victims of a Map: A Bilingual Anthology of Arabic Poetry*, trans. Abdullah al-Udhari (London: Al Saqi, 1984), pp. 12-13. I have altered the translation slightly.
3. Edward Said, *After the Last Sky* (New York: Pantheon, 1985).
4. Donna Haraway, "Situated Knowledges: The Science Question in Feminism and the Privilege of Partial Perspective," in *Simians, Cyborgs, and Women* (New York: Routledge, 1991), p. 195.

Prologue

1. *Autobiography: Toward a Poetics of Experience* (Philadelphia: University of Pennsylvania Press, 1982).
2. Lila Abu-Lughod, *Writing Women's Worlds: Bedouin Stories* (Berkeley: University of California Press, 1993), 27.
3. See *Outline of a Theory of Practice* (Cambridge: Cambridge University Press, 1977).
4. See Njabulo S. Ndebele, *Recovery of the Ordinary: Essays on South African Literature and Culture* (Johannesburg: COSAW, 1991). Ndebele writes: "The ordinary day-to-day lives of people should be the direct focus of political interest because they constitute the *very content* of the struggle." See Epilogue note 5 for more about Ndebele's work, which I discovered in the final stages of writing this book.
5. A massacre by an American-Jewish settler of thirty Palestinians in Hebron on February 25, 1994, took place as I was finishing the manuscript of this book. The Israeli army

imposed round-the-clock curfews on tens of thousands of West Bank Palestinians, including Deheishe Camp.

1. The "Living Martyr"

1. Memorandum to M. François Belon, Middle East Department, International Committee of the Red Cross (ICRC), Vienna. At the time he wrote the memo, in late September 1988, Graff understood that the Boston surgical team was "prepared to perform the operation gratis and [was] trying to get their hospital to waive in-hospital costs." As it turned out, neither the transplant nor the waiving of in-hospital costs came to be. Those costs, which in the end amounted to about $70,000, became the one problem that no one was prepared, or perhaps willing enough, to solve.

2. See "Wounded Palestinian Youth in Boston for Hospital Stay," Mary Curtius, *Boston Globe*, October 5, 1988, 3. A fuller text can be found in the Appendix.

3. For the next two years, liquid nutrition would be infused into Mohammad's body through the Hickman catheter with the help of a dropper machine. The catheter would be replaced the following September just before the second Deaconess visit had to be cut short for lack of funds. It no doubt would have been replaced once again had Mohammad been able to return to Boston in July 1990. When, at the end, it was determined that Mohammad had septicemia, it was too late to replace the catheter since other systems had begun to break down.

4. The first Deheishe female casualty in the uprising, Maysoun had been shot at close range with a high-velocity bullet, the same kind used against Mohammad, when she tried to intervene in the arrest of a male friend in the camp.

5. The wire would have been sent at the direction of Dr. Fathi Arafat, brother of Palestine Liberation Organization chairman Yasser Arafat. I report on the circumstances of Dr. Fathi's promise in chapter 4.

6. As it turned out, Mohammad continued on hyperalimentation back home in Deheishe for most of the time he stayed alive; he was the first Palestinian in the Occupied Territories to have lived on such long-term treatment.

7. In an issue of the *Pittsburgh Post-Gazette* I was reading at the time I was working on a final draft of this chapter, I read that the use of a new antirejection drug developed by a University of Pittsburgh team headed by Dr. Thomas Starzl "appears to have made transplants of the small intestine a practical operation" (August 22, 1991). The breakthrough came three years too late for Mohammad.

8. "That Friday [December 16, 1988] was the most lethal since the start of the Intifada," according to a *Kol Ha'ir* journalist. The day began with an early-morning funeral procession for the burial of a fifteen-year-old Nablus youth and ended with the death and burial of five more. Three others injured that day died soon after.

9. See the Appendix for a fuller text of Ori Nir's "The Uprising and the Making of a Hero," translated by the Israeli Government Press Office in "Selections from the Hebrew Press" (Jerusalem, October 25, 1988). The piece was originally published in the Hebrew daily *Ha'aretz* (October 7, 1988).

10. That distance widens over response to the September 1993 Oslo Accords or the "Gaza-Jericho First" option that Damascus-centered groups like Habash's Popular Front see as part of the continuing "South Africanization of Palestine."

2. The Deheishe Story

1. See David Grossman, *The Yellow Wind* (New York: Viking Penguin, 1986), 55.

2. According to the Fourth Geneva Convention, to which Israel is a signatory, residents of an occupied territory cannot be imprisoned in the occupier's territory.

3. See Benny Morris, *The Birth of the Palestinian Refugee Problem, 1947-1949* (London and New York: Cambridge University Press, 1988).

4. In the early morning of April 10, 1948, two-thirds of the inhabitants of Deir Yassin (254 people) were slaughtered by a combined force of Irgun and Stern, Jewish terrorist groups acting in collaboration with the official Jewish leadership (Haganah). News of the Jerusalem-area slaughter spurred the flight of thousands of frightened villagers like those of Zachariya. See David Hirst, *The Gun and the Olive Branch: The Roots of Violence in the Middle East* (London: Faber & Faber, 1977), 124-29.

5. See Kanafani's story "The Land of the Sad Oranges," first published (in Arabic) in 1958, translated into English and collected by Hilary Kilpatrick in *Men in the Sun and Other Palestinian Stories* (Washington, D.C.: Three Continents Press, 1978).

6. For a definition of resistance literature based on the work of Kanafani, see Barbara Harlowe, *Resistance Literature* (Austin: University of Texas Press, 1987).

7. For a fuller text of the letter, see Hilary Kilpatrick's introduction to *Men in the Sun*, 2.

8. The phrase "true Palestine" comes from Kanafani's novella *Return to Haifa*, first published in 1969 and collected in *Palestine's Children*, trans. Barbara Harlowe (London: Heinemann, 1984). Kanafani's representation of what it means to be Palestinian operates as a counterhegemonic force within mainstream Palestinian politics. Since the opening of peace talks in Madrid in the fall of 1991, Deheishe residents increasingly have viewed Palestinian participation in these talks as undermining a "true" Palestine.

9. "Letter from Gaza," *Men in the Sun*, 86. Page numbers for subsequent passages appear in the text.

10. As a matter of historical fact, the Israelis' raid on Gaza in February 1955 was a prelude to their Sinai operation a year and a half later. Nasser's ascendance was a threat that Prime Minister David Ben-Gurion wanted to thwart as soon as events could be made to justify an Israeli attack on Egypt. The anticipated fedayeen activity that followed the Gaza raid was used as part of Israel's justification. For a fuller account of events leading to the Suez War, see Benny Morris's *Israel's Border Wars, 1949-56: Arab Infiltration, Israeli Retaliation and the Countdown to the Suez War* (Oxford: Oxford University Press, 1993).

3. "What Does It Mean Human?"

1. It should be noted that the identity constructed for the sabra, the Israeli-born citizen, was counterposed against Malamud's kind of down-and-out Jewish character, often called the shlemiel.

2. The editor who read this early draft suggested that my readers would wonder why I was talking so much about myself in a story about Palestinians. Although my manuscript was rejected, the question turned out to be useful in positioning my own story.

3. Beit Sahour's merchants refused to pay into a tax fund that only minimally found its way back into the West Bank to provide services for Palestinians; mostly it was used to build roads that would connect Jewish settlements and bypass Arab towns.

4. Feldman's article was translated by Samir Abu-Shakrah and me for the Palestine Human Rights Information Center's *Update*, February 1, 1989. I am quoting from our joint translation.

5. Sometime after Suhaib's release from Makassad, he and his family were awarded a substantial settlement from charges they brought against Teddy Kollek's Jerusalem. Since

then, Suhaib was convicted of the torching of Israeli cars in East Jerusalem, something he could apparently do with his one good arm.

6. See Charles L. Black Jr., Sterling Professor of Law, Yale Law School: "Let us rethink our 'special relationship' with Israel" (Jewish Committee on the Middle East, September 1989). Body count alone cannot measure the communal effect of multiple deaths, as U.S. communities learned during the Vietnam War. Professor Black brings home the cost of the Intifada to West Bank and Gazan communities when he points out that the number of Palestinian casualties during the first two years of the Intifada had the equivalent effect of the Vietnam and Korean Wars combined.

4. Through the Looking-Glass in Cairo

1. The "Desert Storm" operation against Iraq was initiated some ten months later.
2. I discuss Roots's role in Mohammad's case in the Prologue.
3. Neturei Karta has had an official representative in the Palestinian peace delegation.
4. See Ghassan Kanafani, *Palestine's Children*, trans. Barbara Harlowe (London: Heinemann, 1984).

5. First Return: Mourning a Martyr

1. Nahalin is a village of 4,500 located thirteen kilometers from Bethlehem. Its residents compare the events of April 13, 1989, with Nazi pogroms against Russian villages during World War II. This village, along with Batir, was one of the "liberated" villages in the mountainous area just east of the Jerusalem-Hebron Road not far from Deheishe. Having withstood repeated army raids, Nahalin was "an intolerable challenge to the Israeli authorities" and likely chosen as an example in a surprise raid that began at 4:30 a.m. with the shooting in all directions of live ammunition by up to two hundred soldiers and border police. Five persons were killed that day and upwards of eighty-five were injured. The Palestine Human Rights Information Center published an extensive report on the massacre in its May 1, 1989, *Update*, 143-48.
2. See *Update*, May 1, 1989 (Chicago and Jerusalem: Database Project on Palestinian Human Rights).
3. Reported in their monthly *Information Sheet*, April 1990, 23, by B'tselem, an Israeli human rights center organized in response to increased human rights violations against Palestinians during the Intifada.
4. Ibid., 24.
5. Ibid.

7. Third Return: Violating and Transforming Space

1. See "Torture and Intimidation in the West Bank: The Case of Al-Fara'a Prison," International Commission of Jurists and Its West Bank Affiliate, Law in the Service of Man (Al Haq). The undated publication was purchased at Beir Zeit's Book Fair June 26, 1990.
2. Ibid.
3. See *Beyond the Veil: Male-Female Dynamics in Modern Muslim Society* (Bloomington: Indiana University Press, 1987).
4. Quoted by Yacov Ben Efrat, "A Deal, Not Peace," *Challenge: A Magazine of Israeli-Palestinian Coexistence* 4, no. 5 (September-October, 1993): 10.

Epilogue

1. Jean Genet, *Prisoner of Love* (Middletown, Conn.: Wesleyan University Press), 231. Page numbers of subsequent citations appear in the text.

2. Bourdieu, *Distinctions: A Social Critique of the Judgement of Taste*, translated by Richard Nice (Cambridge, Mass.: Harvard University Press, 1984), 474.

3. "Not You/Like You: Post-Colonial Women and the Interlocking Questions of Identity and Difference," *Inscriptions* 3/4 (1988): 71-77.

4. Again, I am indebted to Njabulo Ndebele, whose corroborating work on the "ordinary" I discovered as I was crossing yet another set of borders and once again recollecting myself a long way from home as a Fulbright scholar at Rhodes University in the South African summer (February) of 1994. This writer and cultural critic explores in both his essays and his short stories what he calls the "mechanisms of survival" by which black South Africans were able to live under the harsh conditions of apartheid. In defining the task of "a new generation of South African writers" in the building of "a new creative, and universally meaningful civilization . . . in South Africa," Ndebele instructed them "to look for that area of cultural autonomy and the laws of its dynamism that no oppressor can ever get at, to define that area, and, with purposeful insidiousness, to assert its irrepressible hegemony during the actual process of struggle." (*Recovery of the Ordinary: Essays on South African Literature and Culture* [Johannesburg: COSAW, 1991], 159).

I find such an area of autonomy explored in the stories of Ghassan Kanafani as well as enacted in Deheishe's struggle to maintain dailiness and the ordinary under the Occupation. Kanafani and Deheishe, in fact, have shed light on one another.

5. That collaborators have been ordered by Israeli security to place innocent Palestinians like Nidal's friend under suspicion for just such demoralizing effects as Deheishe was experiencing was reported in a leaflet that was smuggled out of Megiddo prison in 1990 by Palestinian prisoners who had interrogated a known collaborator.

6. Palestinians opposed the accords because they were neither consulted in the writing of them nor recognized as a people in the wording except as a "refugee problem."

Index

Compiled by Eileen Quam and Theresa Wolner

Janet Varner Gunn is currently teaching in the Department of English at Rhodes University, South Africa, where she was a Senior Fulbright Lecturer in 1994. Prior to going to South Africa, she was a research associate in women's studies at the University of Pittsburgh and, before returning to Jerusalem, she was chair of religious studies at the University of North Carolina at Greensboro. She is the author of *Autobiography: Toward a Poetics of Experience* (1982) and publications on Rigoberta Menchú's *testimonio* and Palestinian Leila Khaled's autobiographical manifesto. She is working on a project she calls "survivor knowledge" that will take her back to an earlier interest in Holocaust memoir as well as into South African testimonials on what Njabulo Ndebele calls the "mechanics of survival" under apartheid. *Second Life* is her first book-length attempt at autobiographical writing.

Lila Abu-Lughod is associate professor of anthropology at New York University. Her areas of research include social anthropology, gender studies, popular culture, third world media, social transformation, politics of scholarship, Islam, and the Middle East.